The Culture of God

The Syrian Jesus –
reading the divine mind,
sailing into the divine heart

Nadim Nassar

- (possibility of) Reconciliation of god + one another if life and teachings of Christ are truly lived

- Paradox of Crucifixion + Christianity = key to understanding restoration of same Humanity.

HODDER

First published in Great Britain in 2018 by Hodder & Stoughton
An Hachette UK company

This paperback edition first published in 2019

1

Copyright © Nadim Nassar, 2018

The right of Nadim Nassar to be identified as the
Author of the Work has been asserted by him in accordance
with the Copyright, Designs and Patents Act 1988.

Unless indicated otherwise Scripture quotations are taken from the
New Revised Standard Version of the Bible, copyright © 1989 by the Division
of Christian Education of the National Council of the Churches of Christ in the USA.
Used by permission. All rights reserved.

All rights reserved. No part of this publication may be reproduced,
stored in a retrieval system, or transmitted, in any form or by any means
without the prior written permission of the publisher, nor be otherwise
circulated in any form of binding or cover other than that in which it is published
and without a similar condition being imposed on the subsequent purchaser.

A CIP catalogue record for this title is available from the British Library

Paperback ISBN 978 1 473 67154 6
eBook ISBN 978 1 473 67155 3

Typeset in Sabon MT by Palimpsest Book Production Ltd, Falkirk, Stirlingshire

Printed and bound in Great Britain by Clays Ltd, Elcograf S.p.A.

Hodder & Stoughton policy is to use papers that are natural, renewable
and recyclable products and made from wood grown in sustainable forests.
The logging and manufacturing processes are expected to conform
to the environmental regulations of the country of origin.

Hodder & Stoughton Ltd
Carmelite House
50 Victoria Embankment
London EC4Y 0DZ

www.hodderfaith.com

Contents

إليكِ أمي ..
عندما تلمس شفتي وجنتيك أمي، أعرف أني قد قبّلت هدب الله

To you, my Mother.
When my lips touch your cheek, Mum,
I know I have kissed the garment of God.

'I call you friends, because I have told you everything
I heard from my Father'.
John 15:15

I first met The Revd Nadim Nassar when he came to dine with HM The Queen at Windsor Castle in 2016. After the meal, we talked at length about his work, especially his ministry with the children and young people of Syria. Shortly after, I visited the Awareness Foundation to meet Nadim's team and learn more about their ministry. I was so moved by their programmes which spread peace around the world that I accepted Nadim's invitation to become the Awareness Foundation's Royal Patron.

Nadim brings a unique perspective. As the first ever Syrian to become a priest in the Church of England, Nadim has devoted his life to bringing the region of his birth and his adopted home-land ever closer together. An important element of this has been to remind Christians around the world that theirs is a Near Eastern faith, full of Near Eastern culture and symbolism.

In this book, Nadim tackles this very subject, allowing those who are not from the Near East a rare glimpse into the earthly culture that Christ himself loved and live. The culture of God, which is the culture of Love, is a ground-breaking idea. The lessons that Nadim shares from his personal life as well as his journey of exploration into this exciting culture should resonate with us all. In completing his first book, Nadim has accomplished a lifelong dream – a dream which he shared with me when I become Patron of his charity. I am delighted to have been one of many who have accompanied Nadim on this virtual pilgrim-ages, from the initial ideas which took years to gestate until the writing process enabled him to share this with us all.

HRH The Countess of Wessex GCVO

Introduction by Revd Dr Habib Badr

A British public servant once wrote: 'I lived and worked for thirty years in India, during which time I learnt a great deal about England!' This reflects Nadim Nassar's deeply personal and profoundly evangelical account of his understanding of the culture of God. Nadim grew up in the Levant – that is, the Middle East. His experiences as a child and teenager in Syria followed by seven years of study in Lebanon, form the basis of his observations and insights. However, these experiences became meaningful and defining for his life and thought only *after* he left the East altogether to further his studies in Germany, and later live and work in the United Kingdom. From this 'geo-cultural' metamorphosis and transition this book was born.

Nassar states from the outset that the 'divine culture' is fundamentally *Trinitarian*, grounded in a relation of love between Father, Son and Holy Spirit. And although for Christians the Trinity is essentially a great mystery of faith, because of God's coming down to that part of planet earth known as the Levant, we human beings are now able to glimpse the culture of God by coming to a better and deeper knowledge of the life and work of Jesus of Nazareth. Nassar further claims that the Levantines are at a slight advantage in this regard because they are better equipped to understand the indigenous culture of Christ, and therefore to interpret it to the rest of the world. He also suggests that 'orientalists' such as himself, who have lived in the West for some time, and therefore understand both their own culture as well as that of the West, are especially poised to offer such an understanding and interpretation.

The Levantine insights that Nassar offers the reader into the nature, life, works, teachings and parables of Jesus are rich, refreshing, deep, creative and efficacious. This book, therefore, is essentially a wonderful and rich companion to the four Gospels. Its chapters follow, more or less, the life of Jesus, and slightly beyond, to the life of the apostles. In every case Nassar, out of his personal experiences in the East and the West, penetrates the biblical texts, offering a profound and creative understanding of the Trinitarian culture of God.

I especially enjoyed, and was deeply moved, by chapter 8, which deals with the crucifixion and resurrection of Christ. I specifically invite the reader to carefully absorb the last section on *forgiveness*. It is most moving and powerful – especially as the author relates it to his own personal experience with violence, bloodshed and death in his Levantine context and today's world. To entice the reader, I will say that, for me, it came as 'good news!' indeed to learn that 'love and forgiveness are integral not only to God's commandments, but to the inner life of the Trinity.'

At the book's close the author strikes a hopeful and joyful note. 'In the Resurrection of Christ,' Nassar sees 'the ultimate manifestation of the culture of God as the culture of eternal life. It is the culture that changed our cultures radically by giving us the possibility of exploring the mind, the heart and the passion of God.'

This book contains a reservoir of great sermons. And, if you are looking for a better understanding of the Christian faith, and a down-to-earth interpretation of what it means to be a Christian today, this book is for you. For, as Nassar himself tell us, 'through taking the journey of Jesus, from his birth to the Resurrection ... we gain real access to the culture of God.' And, if as a twenty-first-century citizen of this world you are confused, pained and disturbed by the terrible phenomena of terrorism, suicide bombings, radicalization and extremism, this book is a must-read, because it will show you a way forward, offering a realistic alternative and a useful roadmap toward a brighter future of reconciliatory action, dialogue and peace-making.

Revd Dr Habib Badr
Beirut, July 2018

A Word from the Author

'When did you become a Christian?' This is the question I have been facing for the last twenty years, living and working in London. Most of the people suppose that because I come from Syria, I had to be Muslim and converted to Christianity. When I say that I have always been a Christian, then the next assumption is usually that my parents converted to Christianity. A lot of people find it difficult to believe that my family have been Christian for generations, perhaps all the way back to the time of St Paul. People in the West forget that Syria and the Levant region were Christian for more than 600 years even before Islam started. Before the rise of ISIS in the Levant, and the severe persecution of the original Christians in the region for the last five years, Christians in the Near East have been almost invisible to the West, and to Western Christians.

Such ignorance has left the churches in the West totally confused about how to help Christians and churches in the Levant during this terrible time of war and violence. The vast majority of the help sent to the region has been humanitarian; this is of course very important, but the Christians in the Near East don't need blankets, tents and food. They need recognition, and they need spiritual, moral and existential support. The number of Christians in the region is decreasing dramatically as many of those who can leave the Near East have done so – or they are waiting for a visa from another country.

Every single Christmas, in every single church around the world, we read Luke chapter 2:1–2, 'In those days a decree went out from Emperor Augustus that all the world should be registered. This was the first registration and was taken while Quirinius was governor of Syria.' But who stops and asks why Luke would mention the governor of Syria, and why was this relevant to the birth of Jesus? It is very relevant, because where Jesus was born was a satellite of the great Roman province of Syria. In other words, Jesus was a Syrian!

There is a saying in English, 'I have had a "road to Damascus" experience.' Most of those who use this saying don't know its origin. Even many of those who do know that this phrase refers to the conversion of Saul to Christianity and his becoming Paul on the road to Damascus still do not associate this Damascus with the capital of Syria today. Unfortunately, in the West, Christianity has become Western and the places in the Bible have become a historical fantasia. I have always reminded the British that they look at Damascus like Camelot, a bit of history mixed with a lot of fable and legend. What many do not know is that, if you travel to Damascus today, you can still walk along the 'street called Straight', which the Lord himself spoke of when he commanded Ananias to go and find Paul (Acts 9:10–19). You can also still find the place, in the street called Straight, where Paul was baptised and the wall in Damascus where 'his disciples took him by night and let him down through an opening in the wall, lowering him in a basket' (Acts 9:25).

Having said that, in the Near East, many Muslims and non-Christians view Christianity as a Western import, and this is very strongly associated with colonialism. They forget that Christians have played a major role in the whole history of the region, including a significant role in defeating the Crusades, and in ending the French and British occupation.

All of this led me to work hard to dispel ignorance between East and West, not only regarding Christianity as a faith, but also the effect of this ignorance on cultural, economic and political relationships between the regions. I have written this book as a step on the journey to raise awareness about the essence of Christianity and its relationship with the original culture of the New Testament, which is Levantine or 'Near Eastern'. I have done my best to link this with my own life and experiences in the region, as a Syrian who grew up in an environment surprisingly similar to Jesus' own. Whether we are Christians or not, we cannot understand Christianity unless we understand Jesus, who revealed the culture of God in his own earthly culture. I do hope that as you read this book you will gain a deeper appreciation and understanding of the person, life and teachings of Jesus Christ, and that through this you will embrace and claim the treasure that he brought to share with us.

Finally, I should express my deep gratitude to all who have helped me in the exciting process of writing this book, especially my dear friend and colleague St John Wright; I am also grateful for the support and encouragement of my family and friends, including Tony Whittingham in Canada, Stuart Wolfendale in Hong Kong, and David Goymour in London, as well as my colleagues at the Awareness Foundation. I am so grateful to my editor, Katherine Venn at Hodder, who convinced me to write the book and who guided me painlessly through the publication process.

Nadim Nassar
London, June 2018

I

Cultures of Death, Cultures of Life

Over the last sixty years, the Middle East has been consumed by the fires of war and sectarian hatred. In my short life I have lived through four major wars, beginning with the Six Day War in 1967, which opened the floodgates for violence and open warfare between Israel and its Arab neighbours. In 1973, the Yom Kippur War was the first to leave a major scar on my soul; my Syrian hometown, Lattakia, was bombed by Israel and, for three days, night turned into day as huge oil tanks burned close to my home. I heard the bombers overhead, and my house was shaken by the explosions that followed. I remember that, every night, I would sit on my mother's lap for hours, shaking in fear. The sound of an air-raid siren still sends a chill through me. For years after this there would be occasional Israeli air attacks, which perpetuated the sense of terror.

Growing up as a Christian, at an early age I wanted to study to be a priest. In 1981, aged seventeen, I travelled to Lebanon's capital, Beirut, to study at the only Protestant school of theology in the Levant – what is called, in the West, the Near East. The Lebanese Civil War had started in 1975, but without understanding what living through a civil war would actually mean I insisted on going. The seven years I spent in Beirut, from 1981 to 1989, completely reshaped my personality; I lived so close to death throughout that time. We took turns to guard the school by stationing ourselves at the reception desk. I remember one day two heavily armed militia fighters coming into the school. They were retreating and wanted to cross the school grounds and leave via the back. I was working at reception with an older Lebanese student. We had to stop them and insist that they went back the way they had come; otherwise, the other militia would have pursued them, probably with grenades. The school would have become a battleground. The two fighters could have killed us, but we asked them not to jeopardise the lives of the many who were hiding in the school's basement. Finally, they were convinced and left.

I am sure many people have very happy memories of their time at school or university, relaxing or studying in the quiet calm of the library. We literally had to crawl into the library to fetch books because snipers were watching every window. Despite our best precautions, no one could truly be safe. Early during my time at the school, one of my fellow students was killed by a sniper's bullet to the brain.

When a battle started around the school of theology we would rush to the basement and stay there, sometimes for a week or ten days, living on a very limited amount of food and water, waiting for it all to end. After each battle finished, we would emerge from the basement and our first question was always, 'Which militia is in charge of our area this time?' At different times we were controlled by the Druze Militia, the Muslim Sunni Militia, the Christian Phalangists, and even the National Syrian Socialist Party. In 1982, during the Israeli occupation of Beirut, an Israeli tank entered our school yard, pointing its main gun at our building because the crew thought the people in the basement were fighters rather than theology students!

Many times I saw priests sticking posters of Christ and the Virgin Mary on tanks, and sprinkling those tanks with Holy Water. I saw every religion abuse their faith in that war. The militias had political names, but their identity was inevitably sectarian. Each group believed that they were fighting for their existence in Lebanon, and for the survival of their beliefs. The horrible thing is that those sects were able to convince so many young men and women that they were fighting for a just cause, and that their fight was existential. It was painful to see how political interests and ideologies not only abused religion, but also thrived by making religion the essential point of that war. Through this hell, those sects persecuted and massacred each other. The more persecution and massacres, the more people believed that this was a fight to the death. People who had lived side by side for generations, in cities, towns and villages, suddenly desired nothing but the annihilation of every neighbour who was in any way different.

I remember travelling from West to East Beirut, crossing the Green Line to meet my cousin, whom I hadn't seen for five or six years. I travelled in an ambulance under a sheet, pretending to be injured. If I had been discovered, my Syrian accent would have cost me my life.

If religion was truly the deepest purpose of this war, then how could the Near East School of Theology – which trained the whole region's Christian leaders – survive deep in the heart of the so-called 'Muslim area' of Beirut, West Beirut?

I remember the last big battle. When we emerged from the storm, we walked around the school to see the aftermath and to check the building. Destruction was everywhere. A car was teetering on the balcony of the second floor of the building next to us. Houses and shops were on fire, rubble filled the streets. Bodies of fighters and civilians lay around. Yet somehow, the next day, people would carry on their lives as before – as best they could.

In the middle of this 'culture of war and death', I somehow also experienced a vibrant 'culture of life' that expressed itself through theatre, art and books. I had never experienced this before. I had always been interested in art and culture when I lived with my family, but in Lattakia cultural life was extremely limited. In Beirut, even during the war, I started attending cultural events and exhibitions and going to the cinema. Beirut had been

Beirut

known as the Paris of the Orient, and its cosmopolitan lifestyle and vibrant cultures, together with a freedom rare in the region, meant that this was an exciting world to explore. Always in a time of war, a time of death, people cling to life in all its forms. The West experienced this in both world wars, and the Levant is no different.

During this time the Protestant churches in Beirut came together to form a new youth ministry as a response to the war taking such a terrible toll on their young people. I was approached by the Revd Dr Habib Badr, my teacher and mentor at the Near East School of Theology, to lead the ecumenical Protestant youth group. This group was to meet at my college; I was only a couple of years older than the young people I was leading. We began with five people, meeting and praying, talking about all kinds of things – especially facing the issues that war was throwing at us: violence, faith, God. With the youth group, I was pushed to think outside my limited background and find ways to engage with those young people and organise activities; they used to come every Saturday, even under shooting and shelling. Were we mad? They came religiously every Saturday afternoon. The group grew and grew, from five to seventy. We created a counter-culture to the war around us by opening up a public discussion about Christianity and violence. We even managed to publish the first Christian youth magazine in the region.

All this made me think about God and life, war and death, killing and surviving, at a very early age. I also experienced how a group of young people could be transformed into a fantastic force for peace around them, making a difference to their environment and immediate culture. My work with the youth group opened up for me new interpretations of the Bible, theology and even my personal faith. I used to have my theology lessons on Tuesday and Thursday, then on Saturday I would turn the theology lessons into a talk for the youth group. This completely changed the way I thought. I would go to one of my teachers, Dr George Sabra, to discuss with him what I would say, and he would help me. It gave me the ability to translate my theology classes into a form of theology that transforms people.

When I graduated, I felt that God had spared my life miraculously; I could have been dead many times over in the seven years I spent in Beirut. Since then, I feel that every day is a gift from God and that God is calling me to spread the peace that I always longed for.

Unfortunately, the Civil War in Lebanon repeated itself in Syria, which began in 2011; my own country had to live through the war I has experienced and dreaded in Beirut in the 1980s. Now, in the second decade of the new millennium, it seems that nothing has changed and we are still able to kill each other – and manipulate God and use him in our ideology and propaganda. Sectarianism was at the heart of the Lebanese Civil War; religion was hijacked by politics and ideologies then, and it seems that this is the raw nerve in the Levant. Again and again, the people of that region fail to control themselves when it comes to religion. We allow people to hijack, manipulate and use religion to kill, to wage war and to gain political power. Over the years, I started thinking about how religion and sectarianism can profoundly influence our cultures, and how profoundly we, as Christians, are ignorant about the best model that God has given us to build our relationships: the Trinity. It is a concept that we do not have the courage to engage with on a popular level; we keep it as an academic subject. How we can base our culture, our Church and our relationships on the culture of the Trinity is just not discussed.

My personal experiences took me on a journey to understand cultures and how they develop. In my region, an understanding of culture has always been tainted by the suffering and bloodshed that has washed the Levant since ancient times. I wanted to look beyond this suffering to a model of culture that could give me hope. Thinking outside my own experience, I wanted to see how to understand the concept of culture itself. What is culture? The simplest form I could identify was that it is the outcome of the interaction of a group of people living in a certain time and place.

If we take the culture of my current homeland, the United Kingdom, we can see that this includes the language and the idioms that the people use. There is also the political system; a long history of creativity in literature, films and music; food (fish and chips, for example); and nuances in behaviour such as where to stand on an escalator – all uniquely British. Go to France, or the United States, China or India, and you will find similarities, but also many differences. Every culture is unique, even though we share some elements and even borrow them from each other. How did the UK end up with its culture? It's not the result of a conscious decision. Rather, the people who have lived in this land for many centuries, either born here or coming here by choice, have coexisted. As they lived together, traditions developed by accident or by design, parts of the culture were celebrated or dropped, and eventually what is now seen as 'British culture' formed. In a hundred years, that culture will have changed again, while keeping much of what I recognise today. In essence, culture remains the product of the continuous interaction of people wherever they may be.

If this understanding of culture is correct, then my thoughts and prayers naturally lead me to the Trinity. I shall explore the idea of the Trinity in much more detail a little later, but for now I will just say that it is the three persons of God – Father, Son and Holy Spirit – in one essence, which is Love. If you are not very familiar with the Trinity as a theological idea, please rest assured that Christians believe in only one God, not three! Now, isn't it obvious that the interactions of Father, Son and Holy Spirit, living together since before the beginning of what we would understand as 'time', would produce a culture of their own? This was the beginning of my quest for the culture of God.

If we have faith, we must nurture it, and increasing our understanding is a major element in growing our faith; only then can we have a full relationship with God. St Paul describes faith as a growing entity similar to a human being, 'And so, brothers and sisters, I could not speak to you as spiritual people, but rather as people of the flesh, as infants in Christ. I fed you with milk, not solid food, for you were not ready for solid food' (1 Corinthians 3:1–2). If we want our relationship with God to grow well, we need to get to know him better; we need to understand and open ourselves to the Scriptures, which are the main source of our faith and beliefs. As we do this, we need to understand three cultures, which I will unpack throughout this book. First is *the culture of the texts of the Scriptures*, upon which we rely for our theology. The Bible as we know it is not a 'book'; it is a library of 'books', and each has its own author, context, culture and audience. Understanding the culture of the text allows us to handle the Scriptures correctly, and to avoid using the verses of the Bible like ammunition in a machine-gun, where all we have to do is fire off an apposite verse and we have 'won the argument'. The Bible does not work like this. The authors' intentions were not to provide us with a catalogue of perpetual statements of truth, phrases that could not be interpreted but should be merely applied like laws. No book in this 'library' is beyond our scrutiny, criticism and interpretation. Jesus did not write a book himself – perhaps because we would have become imprisoned in those words.

The second culture we need to understand is *our own culture or cultures*. It is extremely important to understand the culture we live in. For example, I was born and grew up in Syria, I lived in Lebanon for eight years, I went on to live in Germany for almost a decade, and now I have been living in London in the United Kingdom for more than twenty years. Each place has its own cultural context. We need to understand where we are living, and who we are. We need to understand our roots, which lie at the heart of our identity, and the culture where we live, the culture in which we practise our faith. We are all multicultural now. Every religion believes that we exist for a purpose, and that life is meaningful. How can I understand what God wants me to do in my life, and to carry this out, if I do not understand my culture? Preaching, proclaiming or living the gospel depends on our understanding the alphabet of the culture we are living in.

The third culture I suggest we need to understand is the *culture of God*, which helps us to bring the first two cultures into harmony and dynamic relationship. This culture is not directly accessible to us; instead, we rely on someone who experienced and lived this culture first-hand: Jesus Christ. This brings us to the Christian belief that God, through Jesus Christ, became a human being and revealed God's own culture to us in his life and teachings.

We shall draw much from Jesus' life and teachings as we look for, and into, the culture of God. Everything good, all values and virtues, flows from this culture, although we do not connect the two. In the following chapters, I shall take you on a journey, unfolding the culture of God as we look at the life, teachings and personality of Christ, and how his message has had an impact on the world.

2

Glimpsing the Culture of God

To glimpse the culture of God, as I said at the end of the previous chapter, we are fortunate to be able to depend upon Jesus Christ, who experienced and lived this culture first-hand. This assumption, that Jesus Christ lived and experienced the culture of God, comes from a doctrine that belongs at the heart of the Christian faith and all Christian denominations: the Incarnation – which means God, out of his outpouring love for humanity, became human. The implication of this is that all the attributes of God and Jesus Christ are interchangeable. Whatever we say about God also applies to Jesus and vice versa, but we must understand that God the Son, not God the Trinity, becomes human. Jesus Christ, therefore, is in the Christian faith fully God and fully man.

I should like to begin this exploration by considering the two styles that Jesus used when he dealt with people. The first one is *Jesus the meek and mild*, the humble, the loving, the healer, the counsellor – God the forgiver. It is absolutely clear that this is the Jesus who deals with the ordinary people that he meets – the people of his community, strangers, outsiders and even enemies. He healed the centurion's servant, he transformed the Samaritan woman at the well, he raised Lazarus, he healed the woman with a haemorrhage who just touched the hem of his garment, he called a tax-collector to be one of his disciples, he forgave Zacchaeus the tax-collector and entered his home. But we also find a *volcanic Jesus* in the New Testament, shaking the ground under the feet of those in religious power – the Pharisees and the scribes. In Matthew 23, Jesus launches a series of fierce attacks on these leaders:

> 'But woe to you, scribes and Pharisees, hypocrites! For you lock people out of the kingdom of heaven. For you do not go in yourselves, and when others are going in, you stop them.' (23:13)

This saying of Jesus belongs to the essence of the culture of God; here, Jesus is being both ironic and funny, and his audience would have laughed when they heard this. Jesus wanted to speak the truth that touches the people's hearts on the one hand, and on the other, to really strike the leaders. This is how Jesus handled his earthly culture and the culture of God. Nobody now listens to this sentence and smiles – but in the Levant, you would immediately laugh at Jesus' irony.

Jesus then attacks the religious leaders for their flawed understanding of what is sacred: 'Woe to you, blind guides, who say, "Whoever swears by the sanctuary is bound by nothing, but whoever swears by the gold of the sanctuary is bound by the oath." You blind fools! For which is greater, the gold or the sanctuary that has made the gold sacred?' (23:16–17). Here, Jesus is not only using harsh words – this is also an exceptional way of speaking that Jesus used exclusively when he spoke to or about the religious leaders. He did this on purpose, to show without any doubt that the leadership they modelled does not belong in any way to the culture of God.

Jesus is furious with the religious leaders because they place great weight on minor matters while ignoring what really counts; he calls them hypocrites, 'For you tithe mint, dill, and cummin, and have neglected the weightier matters of the law: justice and mercy and faith' (23:23). Hypocrisy is especially loathed in the Levant, and an accusation of hypocrisy would stain someone's character. The power of a person's word was seen as entirely binding and trusted; signatures and documents were not as important as someone's word. So to be called a hypocrite is to be stripped of all trust and decency. Look at how St John writes about 'The Word': 'In the beginning was the Word, and the Word was with God, and the Word was God' (John 1:1). John used 'the Word' because it reflected the culture that he and Jesus lived in, and the value of people's word at that time. The Word is so steeped in the culture of the Levant that John did not hesitate to make it a synonym for Jesus and for God himself.

Above all, it is the leaders' hypocrisy that angers Jesus the most: 'For you clean the outside of the cup and of the plate, but inside they are full of greed and self-indulgence ... you are like whitewashed tombs, which on the outside look beautiful, but inside they are full of the bones of the dead and of all kinds of filth' (Matthew 23:25, 27).

His scathing words of condemnation leave us in no doubt as to why the religious leaders plotted to trap and kill him! Jesus drove a wedge between the leaders and their people, and this infuriated the leaders because their power depended on the people's obedience.

So what is the culture of God, and how can we understand it?

The culture of God obviously involves these two things: God and culture!

First, God. An understanding of the culture of God starts with what is for many the most difficult concept and controversial belief in Christianity: the Trinity. God reveals in Jesus Christ that the Trinity is a relationship, three persons in one. Jesus quotes from the Old Testament book of Deuteronomy when he says in Mark 12:29: 'The first [commandment] ... is: "Hear, O Israel, the Lord our God, the Lord is one."' Jesus calls God 'Father', and Father and Son are both relational concepts (you cannot be a father if you have no children), and the Spirit is the very personification of this dynamic relationship of love between the

Father and the Son. As St John reveals in his letter, 'God is love, and those who abide in love abide in God, and God abides in them' (1 John 4:16).

Centuries have passed and theological debates about the Trinity have never gone away. Thousands of theologians have written thousands of books about it – and no doubt they always will.

So why did I choose to begin explaining the culture of God by discussing the Trinity? Because the very concept of the culture of God depends on it.

There are four important principles to grasp when we look at the Trinity, principles that have been embraced by Christians for many centuries. First, the Trinity is a mystery – we can never fully understand it. It is not a puzzle or a mathematical exercise that needs to be analysed scientifically or a theory to be proved. Remember that Christians most definitely do *not* believe in 'three Gods'; they believe in *one* God, who is God the Father, God the Son and God the Holy Spirit. The Trinity has a strong element of faith – either you believe God is Trinity, or you don't!

Second, the Trinity is not a human invention or a human projection on God. We do not impose a Trinitarian nature on God. God revealed himself as Trinity. In Matthew 28:19, Jesus commands his disciples to 'Go therefore and make disciples of all nations, baptising them in the name of the Father and of the Son and of the Holy Spirit.' Jesus calls God 'Father', and he says to Philip, in John 14:9: 'Have I been with you all this time, Philip, and you still do not know me? Whoever has seen me has seen the Father. How can you say, "Show us the Father"?' On another occasion, Jesus speaks about the sending of the Holy Spirit in John 14:26. On many occasions, Jesus distinguishes between himself, the Father and the Holy Spirit.

The third principle is that if we want to study the person and teachings of Christ and if we believe that Jesus Christ is not simply a prophet but something beyond even that – the Son of God, and God incarnate – then we need to look at the Trinity to understand and appreciate Christ's relationship with God and with us. *We do this by looking for the culture of God*.

Fourth, we need to understand our lives and our reality here and now in the light of the Trinity if we want to take our Christian faith seriously, because the Trinity forms the very cornerstone of our lives, our relationships and the way we understand our existence. We are able to see things differently when we look at them in the light of the Trinity, and we can build better lives and better societies. The Trinity is the ultimate model of fellowship and relationships.

This book is not, however, about the doctrine of the Trinity; so I shall just concentrate on our Christian belief that the Trinity is the reality of God, revealed to us through Jesus Christ, and that this Trinity is One God, Three Persons in relationships of love!

Having looked at the Trinity, which defines the God we believe in, let's look at what makes up culture.

As briefly discussed earlier, culture has many elements, including the customs, institutions, history, language, art and religion of a particular nation, people or group. These elements are formed by people interacting with each other. It is a process. The culture of a society is the product of a group of people interacting and living together; it is what emerges from their common life.

If the interaction of a group of people produces culture, then logically the interaction between Father, Son and Holy Spirit produces their own culture. God is not a super-being living somewhere in the universe; God is the Creator of the universe and he does not live within creation; he is beyond our dimensions, transcending our existence, as our Creator, so the culture of God is inaccessible to human beings. But we can glimpse it through the life and teachings of Jesus Christ, who, after all, came to us from the Trinity. So the culture of God reflects the nature of God, and God revealed his own culture through the life and teachings of Jesus Christ, who is himself the Incarnate God.

The ultimate question of this book is, why does it matter to me, a human being, to know the culture of God, and what impact should that have on my own life and existence? The culture of God is the antithesis of the culture of the Pharisees, yet again and again in the Church we fall into the trap of behaving like them, condemning or excluding others. Understanding the culture of God helps us to uncover the image of God within us, a shining jewel buried deep under the dirt of our selfishness and greed. Rediscovering the culture of God helps us to shine as God intends us to, re-forming our relationships with God and with each other in our amazingly diverse world. The culture of God shows us the ultimate form of loving relationships.

In the light of the culture that emerges from the relationships within the Trinity, we can re-examine our lives, our faith and our own relationships. It is an exciting and also difficult process to unpack the life and teachings of Jesus Christ, searching for wonderful glimpses of this magnificent, life-transforming culture of God. It is like a mirror that reflects our inadequacies, short-comings and failings, but at the same time shows us the richness of God and the depth of his love for us.

'Let anyone among you who is without sin be the first to throw a stone at her' (John 8:7b). Look what Jesus could do with one sentence when the Pharisees came to trap him; now imagine what the whole journey of exploring many glimpses of the culture of God could do for us and our relationships with God and each other!

3

God Embraces Humanity

Throughout my life – especially in Syria and Lebanon, where I lived with many faiths – I have learnt how to relate to people whose faith is radically different from my own. The story of God dealing with those different faiths has occupied a lot of my mind since I was very young. Why? Because I had friends who were Muslims, Alawites, Druze and from other Christian denominations as well. Even in my own family, there is a diversity of Christian denominations. My father was Presbyterian – the church in my hometown was founded by Scottish missionaries – and my mother is Orthodox. The Orthodox church in Lattakia is Greek Orthodox. Most of my father's family are Roman Catholics. It has always been easy for me to feel at home within different churches and denominations. At the same time, I went to different mosques with my Muslim friends. This kind of wide religious experience is not unusual in the Levant. I grew up going mainly to the Presbyterian church in Lattakia, but I visited the Sunday school at the Orthodox church. In the Middle East, people live their religion not only in places of worship, but also in the little details of their lives. My friends would talk openly about their faith, and they would practise this in public; there was no 'private faith'. We will return to this in a later chapter. I have always been fascinated by the ways that people relate to God. In the Near East, we never used the Western approach that, 'after all, we are all the same'; but at the same time, the differences did not create a conflict in society. That said, I was, of course, aware that religion had been manipulated on many occasions in the past to create terrible tragedies.

I have experienced and witnessed incidents of discrimination in my life, but intolerance between the faiths was still rare until the 1980s, when the Civil War in Lebanon developed into a religious war with political undertones. The Muslim Brotherhood, which had been founded in Egypt in the 1920s, started spreading into Syria, promulgating the message that the Alawite rulers there were not true Muslims. They followed this up with assassinations of key Alawite and Christian figures in society. I watched Lebanon and Syria change from places of tolerance and muted multiculturalism to mistrust and open sectarianism as religion became the mask adopted by those who sought political power. Religious identity became a source of power and supremacy over others.

This turmoil in the Middle East, exacerbated by the eight-year-long Sunni–Shia war between Iraq and Iran (1980–88), became a serious challenge for me as I studied theology in the midst of Lebanon's civil war. God's name was being used by people killing each other and committing awful atrocities, all claiming to 'protect' God. Every militia was claiming to be God's Army; I remember the first time I saw a vehicle painted with the word 'Hezbollah', which means 'The political party of God'. People would make a joke that 'everyone in Lebanon has a political party – and now even God does too! The list is complete ...'

I tried to make sense of God's involvement in my reality in the 1980s, and how he could connect with the people around me – especially those who were killing and being killed supposedly in his name. Christians believe that Jesus Christ is the Incarnation of God, and I could not escape the puzzle: what did God, as a man, experience when he walked among us, and how did he work with all our cultures before he became one of us?

I had to go back to the very beginning, when God created us in his own image. Ever since then, he has communicated with us in many different ways that match our ability to recognise and understand him. Because we are created in God's image (Genesis 1:27), we have always had the urge to move closer to him and to know him better. We see the very first fingerprints of God in each culture in the world, through their stories, legends and mythologies – human attempts to answer existential questions very similar to the ones I was struggling with, such as the meaning of life, and who created us and why does this lead us to kill each other in the Creator's name?

Realising this helped me see that God has never stopped communicating with us to reveal himself. He created everything around us – the sky, the stars, the forces of nature – and he gave us our ability to think and ask and wonder! I believe that he always has walked alongside us, accompanying us on our journey towards him, especially through wars and chaos. I believe this because in the light of the Incarnation I can look back and re-evaluate the past. My own existential questions include the meaning of God's own journey to be one of us. Why would he do that when he knew how limited, wretched and messy our lives are? What did the birth of Jesus, which revealed the mind and the culture of God, in one of our human cultures, mean, especially to someone trapped in an inferno of war?

Trying to understand the birth of God in our limited and finite existence, I had to take a journey through the history of God's relationship with his creation.

Human beings first understood God as they understood themselves – as a disparate group of gods and goddesses with different qualities and talents, and with roles and limitations much like their own: so we see a god of war, a goddess of beauty, a god for each element, each trade, each place. We can see this in the Greek and Roman mythologies, as well as in the Near East and Egypt, even in Mayan and Far Eastern cultures, even though at this time a very limited number of people had already begun to worship one God.

God respected this step on the way to a mature understanding of God and of humanity. We were not yet ready for receiving

God among us, even through the sending of prophets or divine laws.

Over time, humanity began to develop an appreciation of God, based not on imagination and conjecture – what we project onto God – but on God's own revelations to us beyond the creation. Monotheism developed gradually, from Akhenaton in Egypt rejecting the idea of a 'Chief God among gods' and believing in an abstract God hidden by the sun, to the people of the Hebrew Scriptures, who struggled to see the contradiction between having a supreme God and having other, little, household gods that were 'God's helpers', known as teraphim (Genesis 31:19; 2 Kings 23:24 and Zechariah 10:2).

As we see in the Hebrew Scriptures, God then interacted with his creation through the giving of the Law, and the prophets; the understanding of the One God was taking on another dimension! Laws were necessary to bring order and stability to society; only then could civilisations develop and grow. God worked through Law because we had developed an understanding of basic civil and social laws. Alongside the Law, God spoke to the people through the individuals we call prophets. These prophets had a special relationship with God, acting as intermediaries to bring to humanity messages of hope, warning, affirmation, correction or condemnation. God's relationship with humanity was still limited – initially through mythology, then through a pantheon of gods and goddesses, and then even through the Law and prophets. Humanity still struggled greatly to understand God and frequently we misinterpreted the Law; we even abused or killed God's messengers because they brought a message which we didn't like since it demanded changes in the way society functioned – and how power was wielded. We denied God's sovereignty, preferring to keep it for ourselves. Humans have always wanted to be the masters of their own destiny! We were not ready to consider that true freedom can be found only in complete submission to God.

Humanity was unable – or unwilling – to see any aspect of

the culture of God beyond who has the power. The culture of God, which is of course the culture of the Trinity and the culture of love, belonged only to God, although he had been revealing glimpses of this culture to us since the creation.

Looking around me in the midst of civil war, I saw how we would have seen this revelation if we had not been blinded by our egos. We can see glimpses of the culture of God even in the beauty of creation and through scientific examination of how creation works, as well as when we read the lives of the prophets and how they submitted to God and received his love and compassion.

After looking back at the human journey with the divine, I had to struggle with the New Testament. In the light of the Incarnation, how could I, in the midst of the storm, understand St Paul when he says, 'But when the fullness of time had come, God sent his Son, born of a woman, born under the law, in order to redeem those who were under the law, so that we might receive adoption as children' (Galatians 4:4–5). I struggled with what 'the fullness of time' could mean when I was in the midst of death and destruction, and why didn't this bring a better life to humanity? Seeing a sectarian war raging around me, I could only wonder how God embracing us had helped us in the slightest!

The best example I can give is when I read for the first time about quantum physics. Before quantum physics, we thought that Newtonian physics could explain the physical world. When I read how quantum physics challenged Newtonian physics with endless possibilities and understandings of existence well beyond anything the older system could conceive of, I felt that I was looking at the meaning of 'the fullness of time' in the middle of the war in totally the wrong way. Quantum physics allows us to look at our existence from a different perspective. For example, in Newtonian physics we live in a limited, four-dimensional existence; quantum physics suggest that we live in endless dimensions. This challenged my limited perspective, which was an angry and negative questioning of 'How could the birth of God "in the fullness of time" mean anything good when I was experiencing such colossal destruction?' Instead, I should step out of my limited 'box' and ask, 'How should I understand the fullness of time and what does God want to tell me about the birth of Christ, especially in the midst of conflict and tragedy?' This reframing of my question helped me tremendously to leave my comfort zone and explore other possibilities to understand my relationship with God even in a difficult, life-threatening environment. God communicates with us all the time, but it is up to us to recognise and understand this. God led me to this discovery; I did not find it all by myself.

My angry and negative state was blocking me from listening to God's real message. But as I started working with young people, exploring the Christian faith with them in the ruins of Beirut, a new dimension opened in my life. My perception of the culture of God grew when I shifted from pointing at God in an accusatory way to listening to what he had to say to me. In time, I understood that being angry with God can be a necessary part of growing into communication with him. What is important is to allow God to reach us in our anger and frustration, to listen for even the faintest signal from him to lead us out of the depths of darkness.

I had to move from dealing with God out of anger, which of course bore no fruit at all, to a more personal and intimate way. My growth came in realising that my anger, while inevitable, was fruitless and was not providing me with any answers. I was angry with God because I wanted him to make me feel his presence in the midst of the carnage, to give me some answers, and yet I felt a vacuum. This made me think that God must have been frustrated that we had been unable to communicate with him through the Law and the Prophets; prophets came with certain messages from God, yet the people rejected them and often killed them. Even Jesus said, 'Jerusalem, Jerusalem, the city that kills the prophets and stones those who are sent to it!' (Matthew 23:37 and Luke 13:34).

But God's love for us was such that he did not abandon us, but instead found a unique way to communicate with us in a more intimate way. This intimacy came through God becoming one of us, and thinking about this made me throw myself into helping young people around me, the people that God had entrusted me with. Looking back, I can see how God used my work with the youth of Beirut to save my sanity and my life in the midst of war, and prepared me to continue the work with young people today in two other countries torn apart by war: Syria and Iraq. Thinking now about my journey towards the culture of God, this intimate encounter between divine and human – God becoming human (the Incarnation) – is one of the highlights of how we can access the culture of God.

In the fullness of time, God revealed to us his radical decision not to send laws and coded messages any longer but to deliver the message himself – he was to be the messenger, and the message, the way and the destination! God wanted to teach us about himself directly, without any mediator. This is the transformation signalled by the birth, death and Resurrection of Jesus Christ, and after two thousand years we still live with the consequences of this event; it was like throwing a pebble into a still pond – the ripples continue long after the pebble has been thrown. In this case, the ripples are everlasting.

My own life in Beirut, and then in Syria and Iraq, has allowed me to witness the depths of cruelty that humans can inflict on each other. I needed to stop and think about the 'poverty' that we experienced in the Near East, not in terms of money, but the poverty of love, of dignity, of coexistence, of protecting the sanctity of human life. We failed to live the richness of our heritage. We fell into a pit of corruption, betrayal and hatred of the other. Our history of dictatorships and oppression culminated in an explosion; this explosion revealed our true poverty. This reminds me of St Paul's statement, 'For you know the generous act of our Lord Jesus Christ, that though he was rich, yet for your sakes he became poor, so that by his poverty you might become rich' (2 Corinthians 8:9). How did Jesus feel when he moved from the richness of the Trinity to the poverty of the broken world of humanity?

The coming of Jesus Christ in a certain time and place as the Son of God, God incarnate, allowed God to experience human existence first-hand with all its limits. God had not been part of his creation; he worked within it, but never as part of it. With the birth of Jesus, he became part of his own creation and at last he experienced what it was to be human. This is almost inconceivable, unimaginable and unthinkable, that God would take a permanent physical form. I have worked for many years in inter-faith dialogue, and I have experienced first-hand that this point is irreconcilable. No other monotheistic religion would allow the idea that the almighty Creator became a human being. What we see as the overflowing love of God expressed through his becoming one of us, is, for others, the greatest insult to God.

For example, in Islam God transcends the material world and any attempt to make an association between God and the material world is an insult to God, in some way degrading him and making him less. This is called *Shirk*. It is therefore incredibly difficult for Muslims to accept that God would, in their eyes, 'lower himself' to become one of us. It is not that Christians associate God with the material world because we wanted to make ourselves equal to God; it is God himself who took that decision out of his incredible love for us.

We have to acknowledge this deep point of difference and choose to build strong relationships with each other anyway!

St Paul's beautiful sentence says that Jesus 'was rich, yet for your sakes he became poor' (2 Corinthians 8:9). How was Jesus rich? He belonged to the Trinity – with all the attributes and characteristics of God – before he became a human being. Jesus the Son of God had lived in an eternal relationship of holy love with his Father and the Holy Spirit. That is how rich he was.

Yet the unlimited and almighty God became a limited human being. The ultimate in holiness was born in a filthy, stinking stable. He walked in our streets, wore rough clothing, choked on the dust from the road, faced the burning heat of the sun; he fasted and he was hungry, tired and thirsty. He built friendships and made enemies, he was persecuted, rejected, betrayed and abandoned; he experienced doubt, temptation, fear, sadness and joy.

God even experienced the ultimate frontier that every human has to cross: death. He allowed himself to be judged and sentenced to an appalling death, nailed to two pieces of wood that at that time symbolised the ultimate public curse and humiliation.

For us, the Incarnation shows that God took a free decision to be like us, to experience personally what we experience in our everyday life. In this, he revealed the culture of God – the richness of God – in our earthly cultures. The point of the Incarnation is God saying to us all, 'I think differently, and I want to share this with you!' God is shockingly different … this most intimate union between divinity and humanity in the person of Jesus Christ changed the relationship between us and God forever. In the Incarnation, God ended our speculation about him, which dominated the relationship between humanity and God, and he showed us first-hand who he is. Without the Incarnation, we would never have had the chance to know God directly as he is. In Jesus, God the almighty, the all-knowing, the omnipresent, the holy, the transcendent, the ultimate force of love, explained himself and his culture of love to us through our limited language and in our limited existence.

As he grew up in one particular earthly culture, he became completely familiar with it so that he could weave wonderful parables that related something of the culture of God to those who heard them.

What are the consequences of the Incarnation, of the Creator becoming a helpless baby in a small town on earth?

One consequence relates to God: the Almighty experienced the weakness of humanity, and that gave God the most intimate relationship with us. After the Incarnation, God's overflowing love now became reality. Think of someone who is obsessed with football; the walls of their bedroom are covered with posters of their favourite team, they have the replica football strip, they watch all the games on TV and they have even been to a stadium to watch a game. What is missing? This person has never even kicked a football! But with the first kick of the ball, their relationship with the game changes permanently. They have gained a direct, first-hand, experience of football and that takes their passion and love of the game to a whole new level of appreciation and excitement. God created us out of his love, and he accompanied the creation throughout history, but he had never experienced what it was to be part of his creation. His love, passion and appreciation of creation gained a completely new dimension when he became a human being.

So we cannot say to God that he 'does not understand us'! When we are sick or hungry, God looks at our troubles in a different light because he has suffered himself. After the Incarnation, our relationship with God has changed because of his first-hand, intimate knowledge of our lives.

The second consequence concerns us. The Incarnation gives us the confidence to say that 'I am significant' because God loves us so much that he became just like us and shared everything we are. Why did God do this? To show us how much he loves us. Now, when we communicate with God we are not communicating with a distant entity that is so transcendent that he could never understand our pain, our fear or our joy. We pray to a God who is close to us, and this should give us comfort, confidence and joy: our God felt, and still feels, what we are feeling.

God revealed that he is not just a 'better' or even a 'superlative human being': he is qualitatively different, beyond time and space, the Creator of the creation, who freely chose to share our humanity. By sharing our humanity with us, he also shared his culture – his mind, his passion, his thinking and his values – with us.

Looking back, I can see now that my journey in the East and the West took me to the doorstep of the culture of God. I felt that God was calling me to open the door! By opening the door, God empowered me to view my whole life in a way I would never have thought possible.

Just as our relationship with God has changed since the dawn of humanity, so should our relationship with each other. After the Incarnation, we should value human life more highly and we should respect each other. If God loved all of us so much that he chose to become one of us, who are we to hurt another human being whom God loves? Each of us has been made in God's image – even those we consider most evil. God's new and only commandment, made while he was with us, is to love each other. This commandment reflects nothing less and nothing more than the Trinity itself because Jesus experienced first-hand the culture of God – the culture of the Trinity, which is *love*. In this way, he was teaching us how to make the Trinity alive in our relationships and this is what we constantly fail to see: the link between our relationships and the Trinity. Remember, the Trinity is not a theory; it is the reality of God and it should be our reality in our own relationships. The Trinity matters because the culture of God, which defines the relationships in the Trinity, is revealed in the commandment that Jesus gave us: to love one another as he loved us. 'I give you a new commandment, that you love one another. Just as I have loved you, you also should love one another. By this everyone will know that you are my disciples, if you have love for one another' (John 13:34–35).

Jesus did not give us laws, books or orders. He did not want to regulate human society as the Law tries to do in Judaism and Islam, where the Law organises every detail of our life in the name of God, and where any failing to follow that Law becomes an offence against God. Jesus did not come to organise our lives or to correct our behaviour with lists of regulations; his mission was to revolutionise our hearts and bring God back to their centre. If the heart is full of the love of God, then everything that flows out of it will be right. Jesus circumvented the laws and regulations and he aimed straight for our hearts – the source of all we do.

Jesus did not want religious law because in his earthly life he saw how destructive this could be, especially when divine law is interpreted by fallible and corruptible religious leaders. Whenever the Church has tried to be legislative, it has failed. This is not what God wants. This marks a key difference between Christianity and both Judaism and Islam.

Religions have a common flaw: religious leaders begin to interpret their divine law in a way that controls their people and ensures their own power. In this way, religion becomes a business, with a market economy where each religious leader fights for their customers! That is how the religious leaders of his own time, the scribes and the Pharisees, saw Jesus – a rival coming to steal their customers, a rival who had to be put out of business.

On the matter of love, Jesus was the most radical teacher in the history of humanity when he said, 'You have heard that it was said, "You shall love your neighbour and hate your enemy." But I say to you, Love your enemies and pray for those who persecute you, so that you may be children of your Father in heaven; for he makes his sun rise on the evil and on the good, and sends rain on the righteous and on the unrighteous' (Matthew 5:43–45). This courageous and daring statement goes beyond human imagination and thought; no religion or philosophy had ever made such a bold statement! Our minds and our cultures have not developed to behave in this way. Only Jesus Christ, the single human who had experienced the Trinity and the culture of God first-hand, could reveal to us how God would think as a human. Jesus Christ is both the link and the contrast between our limited and imperfect broken humanity and the infinite and perfect divine humanity that God calls us to be. Because of that, we can say that this statement shows the passion, the mind and the heart of God and that this statement belongs to the culture of God. Jesus Christ is telling us, through this enormous challenge to love our enemy, exactly how divine humanity, humanity as God intends it to be, would think.

Perfect humanity does not mean that we stop making mistakes – it means that we strive to fulfil the purpose of our creation. Jesus continues to say after those verses, 'Be perfect, therefore, as your heavenly Father is perfect' (Matthew 5:48).

Loving your enemy does not mean emotional love towards somebody you do not like. Jesus challenges human beings not to understand love in the limited way of emotions, which can often be selfish. When love is only emotions and feelings it usually involves an element of possession and ownership; Jesus is challenging us to love without taking ownership because this is the love at the heart of the culture of God. God loved us so much that he gave us freedom, even the freedom to reject him! So when it comes to loving your enemy, this means an active love that forgives and goes beyond merely not wishing your enemy harm to actively helping them when they are in need.

St Paul understood this message, and the depth of the requirement that Jesus made, as love through action rather than through an outpouring of emotion. He wrote, '"if your enemies are hungry, feed them; if they are thirsty, give them something to drink; for by doing this you will heap burning coals on their heads". Do not be overcome by evil, but overcome evil with good' (Romans 12:20–21). Paul, who had been immersed in the Law, could never have even thought this without meeting Jesus on the road to Damascus.

As Paul demonstrated, nothing can compare to personal experience! My experiences in the hell of the Lebanese Civil War in Beirut taught me that even if I had been the world's greatest expert on this war, reading all the books and watching all the documentaries, all this could never be equal to sixty seconds living in Beirut at that time. It gives you a whole dimension of understanding that affects and reshapes all other dimensions in your life. Similarly, when we have those glimpses of the culture of God, this gives us that very dimension of faith that reshapes and re-forms all other dimensions of our faith. Unfortunately, we take a lot of Christ's teachings for granted after two thousand years, and we do not treat them with the level of seriousness and wonder that they deserve.

The culture of God can only be active in our own culture and our own relationships when we go the extra mile through our faith in Christ so that we can understand the glimpses that Jesus reveals throughout his life and teachings. The grace of our Lord is the power of the faith in Christ that enables us to recognise the dimension-changing effect of these glimpses, allowing us to live according to them and thereby exceed the limitations that ordinary human beings possess.

Jesus' new commandment to 'love one another' came to us only because God came to us as a human being and gave us the opportunity to know, albeit in glimpses, the depth of God's culture. This magnificent journey that God chose to take out of love to meet us transformed his relationship with humanity, and it contains within it the possibility to transform our relationships with God and with each other.

God has created us with the very same excitement and curiosity that makes us want to put ourselves in the shoes of others to experience how they live, think and feel. Films, plays and books bring this desire as close as possible to reality as we identify with their characters. We feel afraid as they feel afraid; we are elated when the main character wins through. This is a valuable contribution to our psychological and spiritual development; the ability to empathise is a vital element in the success of the human race. When we look at how God dealt with humanity, we see this same characteristic in God, trying constantly throughout history to get closer and closer to us until he decided to step fully into our shoes and actually become one of us. Later in this book, I will examine how God became our greatest storyteller in Jesus Christ, and how he told stories filled with characters with whom we still identify today.

4

A Man of his Time

I am blessed to come from that region of the world that God chose to live in when he took human form. In fact, I did not appreciate my culture and how much we still share today with the earthly culture that Jesus Christ knew and loved until I left the region to study in Europe. I had the opportunity to look back on my life, and the culture I grew up with, and see them in a new way. In Europe, I was astonished to be asked when I became a Christian. In Syria and Lebanon, where I had lived my life up until this point, I hadn't realised that our Christianity was invisible to the West. I always took for granted that the Christians of the Levant are the original torchbearers of the faith that Jesus started in this area and I assumed, wrongly, that the whole world would know this.

I did not know how powerful the inculturation of faith could be; when I came to Europe, I realised that so many images and interpretations of the person and teachings of Christ are deeply rooted in the West. Even many images of Jesus found in the Middle East are actually Western; we see the blond and blue-eyed Jesus depicted especially in the Catholic and Protestant churches there. Nearly every Christian home in the Levant has a copy of da Vinci's *The Last Supper*, without thinking about how this was a very Italian imagining of Jesus and his followers.

I remember a woman once coming to me after I celebrated Mass at Holy Trinity Church, a beautiful Arts and Crafts

Anglican church in Sloane Square in central London, and shook
my hand, saying to me in a loving way, 'How lovely to have an
imam with us this morning.' I was shocked that she assumed
that I was an imam just because I came from Syria. I said to her,
'I am not an imam – I am a Christian priest.' She responded,
'Don't worry, you are welcome here. It's OK.' I thanked her for
her warm welcome, and explained to her, 'An imam would never
have given you Holy Communion, the Body and Blood of Jesus
Christ. I just did.' Then her look changed from reassurance and
support to utter confusion – I was a Christian priest ... from
Syria?

There have been other, similar, incidents over the years in
Europe and North America, which have made me rethink and
reinterpret the roots of my faith and peel those layers of inculturation of Christianity away so that I could find the cultural
essence of my faith. I come from the same region in which Jesus
Christ lived, taught, died and rose again. I needed to find the
connection between the culture of the New Testament and my
own culture, which is its direct descendant. Thus began a fascinating journey, throughout which the concept of the culture of
God took flesh.

Before we look at the person of Jesus Christ, his life and his
teachings, we should consider the earthly culture in which God
experienced human life and within which he revealed his culture.
It is difficult, and sometimes impossible, to understand the
meaning of Jesus' teachings if we do not appreciate the human
environment in which he taught.

The best geographical term we can use to describe the earthly
culture of Jesus Christ is 'Levantine'. The Levant includes the
modern countries of Syria, Lebanon, Jordan, Israel and Palestine;
at the time of Christ, this consisted of the Roman Province of
Syria and its satellite of Judaea (which included Samaria), as well
as Galilee and the Decapolis (the Ten Cities, including Damascus).

There are many different cultures in the Levant, and of course
every human being brings their own unique interpretation of

their culture. I shall introduce some general characteristics of many of the Levantine cultures; I do not claim that everyone is the same and I do not wish to stereotype any single culture of the region.

To understand Jesus' earthly culture and how he used it to communicate his message, there are four elements of that culture that we need to understand. These are:

- the power of the story and the storyteller in shaping social customs and beliefs, which Jesus used greatly throughout his teachings and ministry;
- the authoritarian religious regime of the Pharisees and scribes who used the Law to control the people;
- the outcasts and the marginalised; and
- the temperament and the characteristics of the Levantine people.

The story and the storyteller

The power of any story lies in the ability to provoke, challenge, move and ultimately transform society, and no stories have done this better than the ones that Jesus told.

Even in the twenty-first century, we are always in pursuit of the story. If we look at the media, whether it is the TV, radio, internet, cinema or periodicals, the story is at the centre. All around us people are hunting for the next story to grab their attention. Every culture around the world has engaged with the concept of the story in different ways; as a result, we have a huge inheritance of mythology, folk tales, histories and literature. We might take them for granted, but stories are at the heart of our cultures and our lives. Stories are such a part of our life; every time people meet, there will always be a story or two to share, even if it is only about a relative or an acquaintance.

Although the mythological heritage of the Levantine cultures is enormous and rooted in a deep history of interaction between cultures, I am using the story in a wider sense, including histories, proverbs, moral stories, fables, parables, epic stories and so on.

People in ancient times discovered the power of the story and used it to explore the most difficult questions. They put their existential struggles into stories – an understanding of life and death, the meaning of their lives, the origin of everything. Stories are expressions of observations, meditations, revealing a deep sense of wondering and questioning. Storytelling then becomes myth-making. There were stories about every little detail of life, such as the ground, the crops, the animals, the plants, the trees, the hills, the mountains, the plains, the sea, the sky, the moon and the stars. The story dealt with every human emotion: anger, sadness, happiness, sorrow, joy, hatred, betrayal, disappointment, guilt and love. It used these details as components to paint a bigger picture, which went beyond people's limited existence, opening up for them worlds of interpretation as they sought their place in the enormousness of the creation, seeking meaning and purpose. Part of this enrichment of imagination came as the characters in some stories were more than mere mortals; they were heroes, demigods and even gods.

People are proud of their stories because they reflect their collective journey, and because they form part of their cultural identity. Stories give people a shared heritage. So good stories are a creative vehicle for powerful communication, and the characters in them can develop a life of their own, coming to embody human traits, virtues or vices; just like the parables of Jesus, they become universal even if they are rooted in a particular culture. Jesus understood this, and when he told stories he did so to create vehicles of the truth. He did not tell stories that merely said 'do' or 'do not do'. His stories are multi-layered, as we shall see, and he was aware of the power that stories could contain, even over many, many generations. His stories redefined concepts and values and went far beyond what had gone before. Even with two thousand years of hindsight, we are still exploring Jesus' parables and finding new ways to understand them. Jesus had found a method that would carry his teachings forever, allowing each new culture and generation to reinterpret them and to discover new depths to the truth within them.

We should acknowledge that cultures that are poor in mythology and stories cannot develop a strong spirituality, because these stories feed into the spiritual life of the people. Religion needs collective experiences of people who have settled in a place and developed a strong sense of culture. The Levant was an oasis of cultures because for thousands of years people had settled there, all of whose cultures had developed as they interacted with each other. Trade, war and friendship helped the kingdoms of the Levant to interact and to flourish. Without interaction, cultures cannot fully evolve. We can see an example of this evolution when the Israelites came from Egypt. They borrowed the name of the local 'chief god', El, and used it as the name of God as they could not speak his real name: thus we have IsraEL, GabriEL, MichaEL and so on.

Everything in our faith started with he who was our great storyteller, through his teaching and spreading the message about the coming of the kingdom of God. Through Jesus, we understand our journey with God before and after. Jesus chose storytelling, and this shows the depth of his knowledge and appreciation of his culture and his tremendous insight into human communication.

Why the storyteller? At the heart of cultural evolution was the storyteller, who remained central in the life of the people in the Levant until modern times. In Arabic, we call the storyteller *Al-Hakawati*. Let's picture the scene:

People ran from every house in the street. The excitement brought them together in the café at the corner. They had finished their work thinking all day about the meeting that evening. Everyone waited anxiously for the event to start and Al-Hakawati – the storyteller – to appear.

Suddenly, a man with colourful clothes and a red hat appeared, carrying a big storybook under his arm. Everybody waved to him trying to encourage him to start reading. Sitting on a high comfortable chair, he opened his book and read from the place where he had stopped the week before …

What is the book? It is not the storyteller's script – he knows the stories off by heart – it is a prop, part of the magic. Storytelling was at the centre of people's lives in the Levant because it inspired them and gave them the heroes, the imagination and the entertainment they needed. The stories were their main link with their heritage and their shared history. Just like the works of Shakespeare, the stories contained comedy, tragedy and history. They provided the people with role models and with important moral messages stressing the value of honesty, loyalty and generosity. Justice ran through these stories, with the evildoers receiving their just deserts and the heroes being recognised and rewarded.

These stories had a captivating power for the people, even though – or perhaps because – they had heard them over and over again. *Al-Hakawati*, the storyteller, fascinated the people with his stories. The people would discuss them, repeat, explain and interpret the stories days and even weeks after the story had been told. They even memorised them themselves. The oral tradition was dominant in the region; indeed, before accessible printing, it was the only way of shaping human values and cultures. If *Al-Hakawati* finished a storytelling session that left one of the heroes in prison or in danger, for instance, the people would go to *Al-Hakawati's* home and wake him in the night and pay him extra money in order to get the hero out of prison so that they could go home and sleep in peace.

In the Levant, the story, *Al-Hikaya*, has shaped the consciousness of the people, and until the end of the first quarter of the twentieth century the storyteller was still the most influential person in the social life of the people of the Levant.

Al-Hakawati had the power to control the crowd through the story. He could excite them, anger them, please them and move them by just changing his voice and choosing specific parts of his story, and recounting its twists with remarkable skill. For example, if two people had had a bad day and quarrelled or got upset with each other, *Al-Hakawati* would have been told about their fight and would make both of them sit on the same side of the café. He would then assign that side to support the hero, who would be victorious at the end. As he told his story, the two sides of the room would cheer their heroes every time they did something great. Finally *Al-Hakawati* would declare the winner of the battle – who would of course be the hero of those two people who were upset with each other during the day. The result would be that the group on the winning side would jump and shout in great joy and hug each other (exactly as people do in a football match after their team scores). This victory of the common hero would bring those two people to come to each other and hug and reconcile and forget what had happened during the day. The storyteller was the peacemaker and the reconciler, building the link between the story and his audience's cultural context.

For millennia people exchanged their stories and carried them forward from one generation to another. They narrated the stories after they had contextualised them and made them their own. Stories reflected their consciousness, psychology and religion. For example, even today we read, interpret and try to explore the meaning of the Mesopotamian *Epic of Gilgamesh*, which is a story that goes back to the third millennium before the birth of Christ.

I grew up in an alleyway in the city of Lattakia, a Mediterranean port in Syria, and I remember vividly my friend and neighbour; his name was Bassam. Bassam was a reservoir of stories, fairy tales and historical tales. I used to love to spend time with him, listening to those stories. Sometimes he would let me choose the story – a great honour. We used to sit in the alleyway, and I would doodle with my finger in the sand while Bassam told his stories. By the way, the sand came from our beaches, not from the desert! The people of the Levant will all have so many memories of these 'grandmother' stories that they heard when they were growing up, and they will retell them to future generations. My life was greatly enriched by Bassam and his stories. My imagination was awakened then, and my creativity now must be the result in part of this time. I see my story as a continuation of the same heritage that Jesus lived, not far away.

Jesus himself was a storyteller who deeply understood his earthly culture, respected its traditions and fully grasped its shortcomings. He had the natural skill to weave parables that were never theoretical, abstract or forgettable, but which made deep and profound concepts both accessible and exciting. He knew precisely how long each story should be, what should be revealed and what gems should be left for the hearers to discover for themselves. Jesus used metaphor brilliantly: when he talked about the pearl of great price to talk about the kingdom of God, or he likened the Word of God to seeds that are sown, he created universal icons of his truth within a single earthly culture. Jesus' parables have almost unlimited depths – whether you are a peasant, a priest or a prince you will always find new ways to understand the parables without losing their true meaning. This is true for people of every culture and time.

Jesus also used different genres and styles of stories – some would be set in the town, others in fields; some were humorous, some were exaggerations, and others were very moving. Jesus dealt with every story like a piece of clay ready to be moulded to suit the moment and context. He knew just which type of story to tell to suit his message, his situation and his audience. Jesus understood the art of storytelling. He got close to the real life of his society. He embraced every aspect of the life of his people, and that was his way to feel the pulse of the daily life of the people around him. He could feel their anxieties, fears and emotional distress, as well as their hopes, joys, dreams, values and most importantly their deepest spiritual needs. He was one of them; he understood their way of life, took part in their celebrations and was quick to help when a healing hand was needed.

Jesus as *Al-Hakawati* took this art to another level. No storyteller can master the art of telling stories without being himself part of his own story and experiencing the highs and lows of life. The power of Jesus' stories was that people felt the stories touched their very existence; they identified with them and they learnt from them.

The Pharisees and the Scribes

Who were the Pharisees? There is a lot more about the Pharisees than meets the eye in the New Testament, especially their thorny controversial relationship with Jesus. Usually, we assume that they were just the higher clergy at the time of Christ, perhaps like medieval bishops. But the Pharisees were more than just clergy; they were also a political power and a leading school of religious thought within the Jewish community, in frequent conflict with their rivals, the Sadducees. Both groups were represented on the Sanhedrin, the Jewish courts. The Pharisees were also a social movement.

The Pharisees uniquely believed that the stringent rules of ritual cleanliness that applied within the temple should also be applied to every aspect of life, even in the street, the home and the workplace. This put a great burden on the lives of the people. Looking at how Jesus clashed with the Pharisees, we can see that these leaders wielded real power with all the trappings of privilege and with real control over the details of people's lives.

In the time of Jesus, although the people resented the Romans and wanted to be free of them, the Pharisees were actively collaborating with them; their power was not just religious but also political. They had even opened the gates of Jerusalem to the Romans and helped in the slaughter of rival factions. This gave them the power of life and death over individuals, stoning, imprisoning or crucifying. While they were teachers who interpreted the holy Scriptures and the religious traditions to their people, helping them to live their spiritual and religious life, they wielded their power, like so many in similar circumstances, primarily so that they could keep it; killing heretics or wrongdoers frightened the people into submission. Sadly, we can see the same behaviour in the history of the Christian Church in the East and the West when religious and political power was combined.

This helps to explain why Jesus was filled with a fierce rage when he clashed with the Pharisees. He saw that they were hypocrites and collaborators, enjoying their lives of privilege while they crushed the ordinary people under enormous burdens in the name of divine law.

The context of the Middle East is not so different today; clergy have a lot of influence over the lives of the people there, and many clergy of all religions are politically involved. Some are working to help their people; others are helping themselves through grabbing money and power.

I should also mention the scribes. They were not a distinct grouping like the Pharisees, but were assorted bureaucrats and experts on civil and religious law, as well as the archivists and historians. They also exercised a lot of power because they ran the courts, as well as being religious teachers, and they were very much in partnership with the Pharisees, working together to preserve their version of Judaism from people like Jesus.

Just listen to Jesus' words to the religious leaders, and see what made him so angry:

'They tie up heavy burdens, hard to bear, and lay them on the shoulders of others; but they themselves are unwilling to lift a finger to move them.'

'They do all their deeds to be seen by others; for they make their phylacteries broad and their fringes long.'

'They love to have the place of honour at banquets and the best seats in the synagogues, and to be greeted with respect in the market-places ...'

'[Y]ou clean the outside of the cup and of the plate, but inside they are full of greed and self-indulgence. You blind Pharisee! ... For you are like whitewashed tombs, which on the outside look beautiful, but inside they are full of the bones of the dead and of all kinds of filth. So you also on the outside look righteous to others, but inside you are full of hypocrisy and lawlessness.'

(Matthew 23:4–6, 25, 27–28)

After we have been buffeted by these outpourings of righteous anger and indignation, we need to think about why only the religious leaders saw this face of Jesus. This furious side of Jesus was never shown in any other encounters in his life, not even during his passion and crucifixion. He faced with silence the cruelty of the crowd who cried for his crucifixion. The few words that Jesus spoke to the Roman leaders show nothing of the anger that he had turned on the religious leaders. He merely reflected their words back to them, making them think about their attitudes and behaviours. Jesus sought to correct those who exploited people in the name of God; he did not clash with the Romans, because he did not want to be misunderstood as a revolutionary leader fighting against the Roman occupiers and he made sure that he gave no signal to the political parties who were waiting to rise up against the Romans. But when it came to the religious leaders, Jesus could not tolerate what they did and said in the name of his Father, and how they abused their stewardship of their faith for personal, worldly power. I do wonder what he would say to the clergy of every faith in the Middle East today, and how he would challenge them.

Jesus objected to how the Pharisees and the scribes led their people because he could see how arrogant and judgemental they were – they did not lead their people with love and understanding but lived separate, privileged lives. The Pharisees held some of the most prestigious positions in society. Even when they walked in the streets they were dressed in their finery – they would have strutted like peacocks. Their leadership was focused on the Law and its interpretation, and in exploiting their people they abused both Law and faith. They abused God, using him solely as a source for their own power over others, and Jesus loathed their hypocrisy: 'Then Jesus said to the crowds and to his disciples, "The scribes and the Pharisees sit on Moses' seat; therefore, do whatever they teach you and follow it; but do not do as they do, for they do not practise what they teach"' (Matthew 23:1–3).

This clash between Jesus and the religious leaders was very hard for him. It was not Jesus' way to be tough or so aggressive, but he had to choose this path because he understood just how much religious leadership could affect people for good or for ill. His relationship with the leaders played a major role in his revealing the culture of God; across several incidents, this clash provided Jesus with wonderful opportunities to demonstrate and elucidate God's own culture. A perfect example of this is how Jesus reacted when the leaders brought the woman caught in adultery to him. I will explore this amazing encounter in Chapter 5.

Outcasts, the socially unacceptable and the marginalised

A crucial part of Jesus' mission and ministry was directed to the people in his community who were least accepted and respected; some were absolutely untouchable, others were beyond any 'acceptable' social interaction. We cannot understand Christ's teachings and the culture of God without examining those people to whom Jesus gave priority throughout his life. His dedication to the outcasts deeply disturbed the religious leaders and Jewish society itself because the religious leaders believed that demonising the 'other' was an essential strategy for preserving Jewish identity and even existence. Jesus broke the social and religious rules and showed the people what in his opinion God wanted us all to do.

Who are these marginalised people who took centre stage in the life of this revolutionary leader, and why were they marginalised?

- The physically and mentally sick were outcasts; we need to understand that at this time medical knowledge was very limited and people did not know how to treat diseases or to avoid catching them. Mental illness was misidentified as possession by demons, and that spelt complete isolation for those affected. There are numerous examples of Jesus healing the sick, such as lepers, the blind, the lame and the 'possessed'.
- Sinners – or those whom the Pharisees considered to be sinners, such as prostitutes, tax-collectors and moneylenders plus anyone who broke any religious law – were looked down upon and shunned. They lived in isolation, socially unacceptable to the point that they would have been prevented from being in contact even with God; the Pharisees controlled the temple, and they chose who was allowed in to God's presence. Jesus was often criticised for sitting and eating with sinners, and the religious leaders tried to use this to alienate the disciples.
- The outsiders, who were called the 'Gentiles', such as the Romans, the Greeks, the Canaanites, indeed anyone who was not Jewish, were considered 'unclean' and there could be very little interaction between Jews and Gentiles. We see this when Jesus interacted with the Roman centurion, whom we shall meet later. Jesus' encounter with the Syro-Phoenician woman is another fantastic example. The Levant has always been a place of cultural, religious and political diversity. People from all over the known world lived together in Greater Syria and in Mesopotamia (Iraq) and for thousands of years different kingdoms and empires rose and fell in that region, from the

Babylonians, the Hittites, the Canaanites and the Phoenicians
to the invading powers of Persia, Greece and Rome.

- The enemies of the Jews were the Samaritans, people very
much like them but who were seen as contaminating the Jewish
faith and identity by mixing with and even marrying Gentiles.
In his memorable encounter with the Samaritan woman, Jesus
broke the rules by travelling through Samaria rather than
avoiding it entirely. At that time, Jews were forbidden by the
Pharisees and other religious leaders from having any contact
with Samaritans whatsoever. There was a great deal of enmity
between the two groups.

- Finally, I must mention that in the community where Jesus
lived and grew up, women were second-class citizens regarded
as possessions that could be 'coveted' by others. Menstruation
was considered absolutely unclean and while they were having
their period women were totally untouchable. A perfect illus-
tration of this is the haemorrhaging woman who fearfully
touched just the hem of Jesus' robe for healing. Behind this
mentality lay the attitude that women were dangerous seducers
who could lead men into sin.

Jesus revealed a lot about the culture of God when he served
these groups, because he went completely against the current,
against the social and religious norm, to help them. He put
himself in a very vulnerable position, leaving himself open to
attack by the religious leaders, who used his actions to try to
turn the people against him. The Pharisees again and again tried
to trap Jesus in his interaction with outsiders in the hope of
discrediting him.

The outcasts and marginalised form the backbone of Jesus'
ministry in the three short years during which he ministered to
humanity. He never turned anyone away or refused to help
anyone, dedicating himself as a living example of what should
flow from a true faith in God. He exposed the way the religious
leaders exploited religion in order to 'divide and rule': how they

ostensibly decided in God's name who was 'in' and who was 'out'; who should be allowed to thrive in society at the expense of the less fortunate. Jesus excluded no one, as we shall see throughout his life and teachings.

The temperament and the characteristics of the levantine people

It is impossible to understand the earthly culture of Jesus without looking at the characteristics of the people of the area, which have not changed much since the time of Jesus. Examining these characteristics will give us an insight into the character of Jesus as well as into why he behaved the way he did. It will also provide the tools necessary to interpret his teachings, which are so deeply rooted in his earthly culture; this is the way to understand the glimpses of the culture of God that are revealed in it.

Passion
Passion is the first characteristic of the Levantine people, and it is at the heart of how I express myself, simply because I was brought up in the Middle East. Often, when Westerners hear someone from the Levant talking they think they are angry, or that they're having an argument. I have experienced this frequently. When I am talking to my sister, for example, or am on the phone to friends or family, people sometimes feel that I am shouting. In fact, what sounds like arguing to Westerners is just passionate conversation – a conversation that includes emotion. In Levantine thinking, we do not believe that bringing emotions to the conversation will in any way cloud reason or suggest that we are losing our temper. We see this as talking with conviction, with our heart, which adds to reasoned discussion. It shows that we believe what we are saying.

The culture of God is love, which cannot be far removed from passion! Perhaps this is one of the reasons why God chose to manifest himself in the Middle East. This quality enriched the way that Jesus opened up the culture of God in a way that people would appreciate, especially talking about love and passion.

Being passionate is very different from being impulsive, although the two could be confused by outsiders. A passionate person is one who has a strong bond between brain and gut, not someone who acts without thinking first. Passion does not necessarily mean a lack of rationality, but rather a wedding of rationality and emotionality. It does not mean losing control! It involves powerful verbal as well as non-verbal, bodily communication, using emotion rather than suppressing it. Passionate people are not embarrassed by their emotions.

A passionate person is called '*shaghouf*' in Arabic; this word comes from the same root as the word '*shighaf*', which means the tissue that contains and protects the heart. Many of us, no matter where we come from, see the heart symbolically as the source of our emotions. When we speak from the heart, it means we speak with conviction, not just that we speak emotionally.

The people in the Levant consider passion a natural way of life – even if their passionate nature can be something of a shock to people from other cultures. For them, passion is the element that gives life flavour, because it saves it from being flat, boring and dead. It is unimaginable in the Levant for people to speak rationally without involving their emotions and passion, simply because this is the way they are. It is their nature, an element of their cultural and psychological makeup. For them, every aspect of culture is intermingled with their feelings and passion.

I never thought of the way I speak or teach or preach as being passionate until I came to live in northern Europe. I have been constantly reminded there that I am a passionate speaker, preacher and teacher. I have had to pause and consider what that means. I had to examine what being a passionate man means, because I was never aware of it. I also have to be careful, because sometimes passion can intimidate people. Most of the time people have looked positively on my passion, especially when it is expressed in preaching and teaching. They feel that it gives the lesson or the sermon a new and different dimension, which helps it reach the hearts of the people listening – not just their minds. Controlling passion should not mean killing its burning flame but rather making sure that the flame does not turn into a consuming fire. Sometimes I feel that passion makes life real when it gets too cerebral or sinks into triviality.

In Europe and North America, people try to allow for everyone's opinion, and surround whatever they say with a bodyguard of consideration for other viewpoints. The Enlightenment echoes down through the last three centuries in the West, and one of its effects is that a false god has been made of so-called reason, pushing emotion aside and marginalising everything that cannot be weighed and measured.

Something that we have always known in the Middle East is that passion and reason can go hand in hand. Sometimes it is reasonable to be emotional. And sometimes it is reasonable to have belief. True reason is a combination of head and heart.

That is the way people have thought for millennia in the Middle East. It is the way it was when Christ walked the dusty roads of Galilee, and it's the way it was long before that seismic moment when God chose to join us at our point of need through the Incarnation.

Hospitality and generosity

Another essential Levantine characteristic, lying at the very core of our existence, is *hospitality*. Part of hospitality, of course, is generosity. The people of the Middle East are so generous. I grew up as one of six children with a huge extended family. All my life in Syria, I remember very well that our home was open all the time for guests, especially for food. We lived near the sea, and I cannot remember a single day in the summer when we did not have visitors staying with us. We used to have a huge jasmine tree in our central courtyard, and I recall that every year we would make hundreds of jasmine necklaces for all the girls and women who lived in our alley. Strangers would knock at our door and ask for some of our jasmine, and we never said no to anyone.

In the community where I grew up, people rarely invited others 'for dinner'; they simply visited each other without the need for appointments, and food would always be on hand in case of visitors. This is nothing to do with rich or poor: food was always available. Our culture was heavily spiced with hospitality and generosity and the sharing of time together. Time for us was never about hours and minutes; it was about nurturing relationships and friendships. Friendships cannot exist without hospitality and generosity.

I did not think anything of this until I left the region and experienced the Western lifestyle. It seemed to me that individualism is much stronger in the West than it is in the Levant, and the idea of community seemed less important. Preaching and teaching in the West, I noticed that many people have become increasingly distant from each other, and that few will stop to help someone in the street. In the Levant, the Parable of the Good Samaritan is about the nationality of the person who helped; in the West, many people seem amazed that anyone helped at all. I have been told that Western societies, such as in England and Germany, used to be much more open, hospitable and generous than they are now. What a shame that things have changed in this way.

So many of Jesus' parables revolve around hospitality because he understood its centrality for his people. He knew that keeping open homes for strangers, to feed and help, was completely usual at that time. Even today, although consumerism and individualism have invaded most societies around the world, including the Middle East, hospitality is still a crucial and extremely vital matter in the life of the people there. Guests for most of the families in the Levant are an essential part of life, and something they take for granted. Jesus not only told stories highlighting this virtue but also lived it himself with the people around him.

There are numerous tales about Jesus receiving hospitality in many different homes and circumstances. In the famous story in

Luke (7:36–50), we see how a Pharisee asked Jesus to come into his home to eat but the religious leader failed to show him proper hospitality. At that meal, a sinful woman 'stood behind him at his feet, weeping, and began to bathe his feet with her tears and to dry them with her hair' (v. 38). The Lord turned to the Pharisee, bearing in mind that all the Pharisees claimed to know and teach the Law and the Scriptures, and rebuked him for looking down on the woman while he did not do the least of his duties towards his guest. Then Jesus praised the woman, who had broken all barriers in order to show him her love and appreciation.

In the Levant, then and now, it is very rude to show the soles of your feet or shoes to someone. The feet are regarded as the dirtiest part of the body, and it was also unacceptable to touch another's feet – or to allow another to touch your feet. The Pharisee denounced this woman and criticised Jesus for allowing her to do what she did, because this was socially unacceptable. However, Jesus considered her action as generous hospitality, which the Pharisee lacked. In this incident Jesus set a different standard and a new definition of hospitality and generosity. That does not mean at all that he went against his culture and traditions; he in fact enhanced the meaning of these virtues and gave them a new dimension – a leap further than people could imagine. We will look more closely at this encounter in Chapter 7. Jesus kept on not only stretching people's understanding of the Law but even revolutionising it completely. We will look at the way he did this, in a way that had never been done before, later.

Another interesting story about extraordinary hospitality is that of Jesus meeting Zacchaeus, a social outcast who climbed a sycamore tree in order to meet the Lord. Jesus sensed the enthusiasm of this man but realised that he was reluctant to talk to Jesus because he felt unworthy. What happened then must have shocked Zacchaeus because Jesus 'looked up and said to him, "Zacchaeus, hurry and come down; for I must stay at your house today." So he hurried down and was happy to welcome him' (Luke 19:5–6). Despite the criticism he faced, Jesus went and received the hospitality of this socially marginalised man in order to teach everyone around him that God accepts sinners who receive God in their lives. Zacchaeus reciprocated Jesus' gesture with an astonishing announcement. 'Zacchaeus stood there and said to the Lord, "Look, half of my possessions, Lord, I will give to the poor; and if I have defrauded anyone of anything, I will pay back four times as much"' (v. 8). This courageous statement was met with an even more wonderful statement from the Lord. Jesus said to Zacchaeus: 'Today salvation has come to this house, because he too is a son of Abraham. For the Son of Man came to seek out and to save the lost' (v. 9–10). Here we see hospitality in its finest form.

The metaphor of banquets and feasting appears again and again in Jesus' teaching. We see it in many places in the four Gospels, including Matthew chapters 8, 22 and 25; Mark 6; Luke chapters 2, 5, 12, 13 and 15; and John chapters 2, 4, 5 and 6. All these references talk either directly or indirectly about hospitality and generosity. It is crucial to study Jesus' approach to hospitality, because it not only reflects the importance of this concept in his life and culture but also unveils glimpses of the culture of God.

In all these examples, Jesus is deeply appreciative of hospitality. He wants to teach us the very fact that his being with us, living in our culture, is an ultimate expression of the hospitality that God shows to humanity. This is mutual; just as Jesus accepted the hospitality of others with pleasure, he offers the same to us. In Jesus, we have entered the realm of the culture of God, which had been totally closed to us before this. God has opened himself and his heart to us, and has given us the possibility of communicating with him directly. In this way, we can be in touch with God through Jesus' incarnation, with no mediator other than Christ. What more hospitality could God show than this?

Relationships

The Levantine people focus on relationships above all else. One way of seeing this is through the Levantine attitude towards time.

People in the West see Levantine people as not punctual at all, placing very little value on the clock. I believed this criticism for a long time and hated the fact that it was apparently true, until I had the opportunity to re-examine my Levantine culture after I had left the region and lived in Europe for a few years. I could then look at that culture from the outside, which provided me with a fresh perspective. It was eye-opening to analyse it in this manner. I discovered that we in the Levant understand time in an essentially different way than people in the West do – and this, in turn, gives us an understanding of how Levantine people understand relationships.

Time in the West is understood in terms of minutes and hours. You may ask yourself, 'How on earth would we understand it in any other way?' I would answer that if you lived in the Levant you would have a different comprehension. People there treat time as a relational concept. How do they do that? Investing energy in being punctual is, for them, a waste of time, because relationships are far more important than schedules. When my friend or a member of my family needs me, everything else can wait because this person in need takes the ultimate priority. While people in the Levant are not punctual, when it comes to their relationships, time become a richly available commodity! In the Levant it is unthinkable not to know all your neighbours.

In the West, many family relationships have broken down dramatically, and society has lost the vital glue that held it together. In the Levant, families do not put old people in homes; our relationships with the older generation last until they die, and their wisdom and love fill the family with joy.

In the West, the first questions you might be asked by someone you meet could include 'Where did you go to school?', 'What do you do for a living?' or 'Where do you live?' In the Levant, the first question is almost always, 'Who is your father?' To place a Levantine person in the right context, you need to know about their family, not their career! Families in the Levant are not limited to the basic nuclear family; the extended family is as important.

This provides a safety net, a support system, and a backdrop to your whole life.

On the other hand, Levantine people can exaggerate the importance of family; it can be smothering and restrictive. In his teachings, Jesus challenged a too-tightly drawn understanding of the concept of neighbour, an essential element of his earthly culture; and he also challenged the over-closeness of the family, because he knew very well that family relationships could be suffocating. Because of this, Jesus challenged the family when he said, 'Whoever loves father or mother more than me is not worthy of me; and whoever loves son or daughter more than me is not worthy of me' (Matthew 10:37). Here, Jesus is not attacking the family, although his words would have shocked and scandalised many. He understood its importance; he called God, 'Father' and, on the cross, he looked after his mother by entrusting her care to his beloved disciple, John. What he is saying is that everything in our lives – and that includes ourselves and our family – must come second if we are truly to follow him. This was, and is, difficult for us all to hear, especially when family plays such an important role in our lives. Jesus' words, meant for all generations, are intended to challenge us even today. But when we follow God, the family will be even stronger, and the more Jesus is in our relationships then the closer those relationships will be.

Use of language

One of the major characteristics of the people in the Levant is how they express themselves. They are always colourful, visual and metaphorical in their self-expression, as well as being passionate. Many people around the world use images to express abstract ideas, but people in the Levant express themselves in a unique way in almost everything they say or write in poetry, stories, politics, religion and even in their everyday conversation. If we look at the Bible, we find it packed with imagery, such as the tree of the knowledge of good and evil, the serpent, God as the good shepherd, and the poetry in the Song of Solomon.

I believe that using imagery makes it much easier to engage with abstract concepts, simply because images are much more accessible. Sometimes when I write or preach I unconsciously use many images, which surprises the Western people around me because the English language is often direct, to the point and simple, while Arabic and other Semitic languages are colourful, indirect and visual. We shall soon see how Jesus deeply reflected this aspect of his culture, especially in his parables.

Many people in the West have relegated their faith to an hour on Sunday morning. In the Levant, it is very different. People there are overtly religious by nature. Every occasion and activity has a special religious greeting or expression; even if you have a haircut or a bath, or you pass by someone who is working, you offer a salutation or a blessing – always including God in it! For instance, if you pass by a plumber or a carpenter at work, you would say, 'God give you health and strength'; if someone has had a shower or a bath, you would say, 'May this bath be as fresh as paradise for you', and the other person would answer, 'May God give you his grace.' This was the situation at the time of Christ and it is still true today; in many ways, the people of the Levant in the twenty-first century are not very different from the people whom Jesus knew and loved.

5

Living the Culture of God on Earth

We find the culture of God in two areas – in Jesus' teaching and in his life. In this chapter, we are going to look at his life.

Since culture emerges from relationships between members of a community, we should look at how Jesus constructed his relationships with his community and, in doing so, how he reflected the culture of God. In other words, we should examine how he linked the culture of God with his earthly culture, through how he related to other people. The Gospel narratives contain many stories where Jesus teaches us that principles and teachings should not only be taught – they should also be lived. He could only demonstrate this if he possessed a deep and profound understanding of his earthly community and its culture.

I have chosen three of Jesus' encounters, each with a different person, to illustrate this. Each left a fingerprint on the memories of the disciples, leading them to record these incidents with great care. Of course, these encounters are only examples; there are many others that we could study to uncover the presence of the culture of God.

The encounters I have chosen are with the woman caught in adultery; Nicodemus; and the Samaritan woman.

The Woman Caught in Adultery (John 8:1–11)

Every time the leaders closed their net around Jesus, they found they had netted a storm that instead trapped them, as we see in this encounter.

Picture the scene. It's early morning in Jerusalem and, in the temple, Jesus is preaching to a crowd. Suddenly there's a disturbance. The scribes and the Pharisees have arrived with a woman who has been caught in adultery. They drag her into the midst of the crowd, right in front of where Jesus is teaching.

In the Levant, especially at this time, a woman had two things that protected her: the first was her virginity, and the second was a man. And that's it. If she has lost her virginity and doesn't have a man protecting her, she has nothing. She is devastated, totally broken. Potentially, she could be a prostitute. Fortunately, this is very far from our view of women today in most of the world, although unfortunately this view does remain in certain cultures.

Now, the scribes and Pharisees are the complete opposite of her. She's broken and they are the strutting peacocks. They have the Law of Moses on their side, and in many ways they embody the Law. They believe completely that they are in the right, and by condemning this woman they are displaying their authority, judges in a self-made court.

But they're not just here to condemn the woman: they have an ulterior motive. They have a plan to trap Jesus so that they can destroy the hold he has over their people. They want to destroy Jesus' reputation and expose him to the crowd so that he loses his followers. Who will control the minds, lives and even the souls of the crowd? The Pharisees see Jesus as a threat to their powerbase and their unique position as the only true interpreters of God's law.

They are convinced that he cannot escape their trap, because they think that no one could understand or talk about God in a different way than the Law suggests. In truth, they were unknowingly trapped within the Law, while they believed that everyone else was imprisoned within it. So the religious leaders approached Jesus full of pride and sure that this time they had got him! What, then, was the trap, and what was it supposed to achieve?

The religious leaders asked Jesus for his advice on what should be done with this woman. If he said, 'Let her go', and forgave her, Jesus would be seen as condoning adultery and, even more seriously, encouraging people to break the Law of Moses; in the eyes of the Jewish people, he would have lost his claim to have authority from God and would have been regarded as little more than a heretic! On the other hand, if Jesus condemned the woman and asked the people to carry out the proper punishment for adultery according to the Law of Moses – stoning to death – he would have appeared to be no different from the Pharisees themselves and his actions would have contradicted his own teaching. The Pharisees would have established their authority over him. Either way, Jesus would have lost his credibility with the people.

So what did he do?

First of all, he did nothing. We often overlook Jesus' silences in the New Testament. He doodled in the dust – something people in the Levant still do all the time. I remember doing it on many occasions myself. Why did Jesus stay silent? He gave these peacocks the opportunity to say their piece, and waited to see if anyone else present (including the woman) would speak up. Although the disciples are not mentioned, they would have been there with their master – but they had nothing to say either. Few there would have recognised the trap laid by the Pharisees, as all the attention was on the woman and on Jesus. Would he condemn her? Would he let her go?

It appeared that Jesus had no way to escape the cunning of the religious leaders. When nobody said anything and it was clear that everyone was waiting for his response, Jesus rose up and spoke. His words made him like a mirror, reflecting the true image of the leaders back at them: 'Let anyone among you who is without sin be the first to throw a stone at her' (John 8:7). Jesus did not focus on the woman and her adultery; he took her completely out of the picture and turned the whole incident on its head, making the self-righteous leaders the centre of attention – now the spotlight was upon them, not the woman, and they were forced to consider their own hypocrisy. This, of course, is how God saw them.

Then Jesus returned to drawing in the dust. When, in time, he looked up, he found himself alone with the woman herself. Even the crowd who had come to hear him had been shown their own truths through Jesus' words, and they had left in shame. Now, at last, with no audience, Jesus was ready to speak directly to her. 'Woman, where are they? Has no one condemned you?' (v. 10). He did not ask if anyone threw a stone – he asked if anyone had condemned her, because the act of throwing a stone was an act of condemnation itself. Of course, only Jesus would have had the right to throw a stone, for only he is without sin. But of course Jesus would not do this. The evil of humanity is our broken relationship with God, and sin is anything that breaks our relationship with God or which pushes us away from God; since Jesus has a fully restored, complete relationship with his Father, that naturally means that he is without sin. Jesus, as a man without sin, who would have been a righteous judge coming from God directly, would of course have been entitled to condemn the woman.

'And Jesus said, "Neither do I condemn you"' (v. 11). This powerful act of mercy and love in refusing to condemn her is equal in power to how Jesus had dealt with the leaders. He condemned the leaders but he did not condemn the woman. He did not try to justify her actions, as many might do today. When the leaders left the scene in shame one by one, they left because they understood exactly what Jesus had said – they felt completely exposed as hypocrites by his words. They had seen themselves through Jesus' response, and they saw their sinful nature. How? They could not stone the woman because that would have amounted to claiming that they were without sin, and they could not forgive the woman because that would have contradicted the very Law that preserved their power. They had been caught in their own trap; all they could do was walk away.

This incident in the Bible was the gateway for me to consider the existence and nature of the culture of God. When I looked at what Jesus said to the leaders, I thought about how many times I had heard this sentence to the point that I had stopped thinking about it altogether. I had assumed that I had learnt all there was to know about these words. I decided to examine them afresh, and I understood that they would never have been said by any human being. I believe that we are unable to think in this way without Jesus' example to guide us, in which case these words belong to no human culture. So where did they belong? This led me to the realisation that they were the product of a divine culture that Jesus had access to, a culture that transcends all our cultures and thoughts. Every day in the Middle East people are killed for their faith or because of the faith of others – the modern variation of stoning to death. The Arabs demonise the Jews, the Jews demonise the Arabs, the Christians demonise the Muslims, the Muslims demonise the Christians and so on. No one stops to think, 'Who am I to demonise someone else', or 'What right do I have to condemn another?' This demonisation brings torrents of blood onto our streets, with many killings provoking retaliations and revenge without apparent end, an unrelenting madness of murder. Just as the Pharisees wielded worldly power through their violent acts, today's violence is manipulated by those who seek the same worldly power. The culture of God stopped the Pharisees in their tracks; today, it could do the same.

Jesus gives us a wonderful glimpse here of how God thinks, transcending mere human judgement. Our broken human nature naturally focuses on the woman. On dozens of occasions I have discussed this amazing event with clergy and with congregations, asking them, 'If I brought you the woman caught in adultery right now, what would you do?' Every time, the answers have dealt with the woman, prescribing treatment such as counselling or rehabilitation, forgiving the woman, or justifying the woman's behaviour. Some have asked, where is the adulterous man in all of this? For us today, the focus on the woman alone has an element of misogyny. In all this, though, we betray our normal and natural, human way of thinking: we put ourselves in a position of judgement or superiority – we offer advice and we interpret the woman's behaviour. But this is not the way that God thinks! Jesus revealed the very mind and passion of God himself: this incident is *not* about the woman, the 'other' – it is about every one of us and how we overlook our own faults and failings in our hurry to judge others.

As Jesus says in Matthew 7:1–5:

'Do not judge, so that you may not be judged. For with the judgement you make you will be judged, and the measure you give will be the measure you get. Why do you see the speck in your neighbour's eye, but do not notice the log in your own eye? Or how can you say to your neighbour, "Let me take the speck out of your eye", while the log is in your own eye? You hypocrite, first take the log out of your own eye, and then you will see clearly to take the speck out of your neighbour's eye.'

This thinking, which might seem very obvious to us today, given that we have been able to read it for nearly two thousand years, is divinely human – this is how God intended us to think. But only a person with a first-hand experience of God's thinking could have behaved and spoken as Jesus did. Please note that human cultures shift and mutate over time, but God's culture does not.

So it is not only that Jesus did not condemn the woman caught in adultery – he exposed our inadequate way of interpreting God. The religious leaders were supposed to teach and to build their society in the image of God, yet all they could teach was brutality and fear built around a violent and vengeful image of God. Jesus had shown the loving merciful God, forgiving the woman while still rejecting the sinful act itself – this is the paradox of being both just and merciful. In this incident, Jesus revealed, in his own earthly culture, a brilliant glimpse into the culture of God.

Nicodemus

The Sanhedrin, the High Council of the teachers of the Law, would have vigorously debated the appearance of Jesus, whom they considered a troublemaker; and as they were trying to determine what kind of person they would be dealing with, and from where he got his authority, I can imagine that their discussion would have been heated – both in the council room and in the corridors of the temple. The Sanhedrin could not decide who Jesus was, and they were unsure whether he posed a real danger to them. As a result, one of them – Nicodemus – had the courage and the wisdom to go and meet Jesus in person to find out first-hand what this troublesome leader was teaching. He decided to visit him late at night so that he could get to know this rising star privately and judge Jesus for himself. He could not have done this openly because his visit would have angered those who wanted to dismiss Jesus and deny him the status of Rabbi; and for a senior leader to go to Jesus to talk to him would also have amounted to a recognition of Jesus and his ministry.

> Now there was a Pharisee, a man named Nicodemus who was a member of the Jewish ruling council. He came to Jesus at night and said, 'Rabbi, we know that you are a teacher who has come from God. For no one could perform the signs you are doing if God were not with him.'
>
> Jesus replied, 'Very truly I tell you, no one can see the kingdom of God unless they are born again.'
>
> 'How can someone be born when they are old?' Nicodemus

asked. 'Surely they cannot enter a second time into their mother's womb to be born!'

Jesus answered, 'Very truly I tell you, no one can enter the kingdom of God unless they are born of water and the Spirit. Flesh gives birth to flesh, but the Spirit gives birth to spirit. You should not be surprised at my saying, "You must be born again." The wind blows wherever it pleases. You hear its sound, but you cannot tell where it comes from or where it is going. So it is with everyone born of the Spirit.'

'How can this be?' Nicodemus asked.

'You are Israel's teacher,' said Jesus, 'and do you not understand these things? Very truly I tell you, we speak of what we know, and we testify to what we have seen, but still you people do not accept our testimony. I have spoken to you of earthly things and you do not believe; how then will you believe if I speak of heavenly things? No one has ever gone into heaven except the one who came from heaven – the Son of Man. Just as Moses lifted up the snake in the wilderness, so the Son of Man must be lifted up, that everyone who believes may have eternal life in him.'

For God so loved the world that he gave his one and only Son, that whoever believes in him shall not perish but have eternal life. For God did not send his Son into the world to condemn the world, but to save the world through him. Whoever believes in him is not condemned, but whoever does not believe stands condemned already because they have not believed in the name of God's one and only Son. This is the verdict: light has come into the world, but people loved darkness instead of light because their deeds were evil. Everyone who does evil hates the light, and will not come into the light for fear that their deeds will be exposed. But whoever lives by the truth comes into the light, so that it may be seen plainly that what they have done has been done in the sight of God. (John 3:1–21, NIV)

When I first learnt English, I struggled a lot because it was almost impossible for me to speak or to write short sentences that were direct and to the point, without imagery or allegory. My English teacher knew that I was gifted in writing poetry and prose in Arabic, but she kept correcting my English and crossing out all the indirect and flowery language that I always brought to my sentences. The Arabic language is full of decoration; we do not speak in a concise, direct way. Arabic is a Semitic language, a sister of Aramaic, which Jesus spoke; all the people of the Levant speak in a very similar way, linguistically and figuratively. The conversation between Jesus and Nicodemus is a perfect example of two people from the Levant speaking to each other. We need to understand this conversation theologically – and culturally. Nicodemus was a brilliant man, a teacher of Israel, and Jesus led the conversation away from the Law and on to the kingdom and the culture of God. Nicodemus knew that Jesus was different, and that whatever he learnt would change his life; he came for a life-changing conversation, and Jesus rewarded him with one that swept him off his feet!

Theologians and biblical scholars agree that Nicodemus was probably one of the most prominent figures in the Sanhedrin. He was very open and clear about their thinking: 'Rabbi, we know that you are a teacher who has come from God; for no one can do these signs that you do apart from the presence of God.' Nicodemus' visit was a fact-finding mission, to find out more about Jesus and what he was up to.

Jesus cuts the introduction short and does not wait for Nicodemus to ask any questions; he heads directly to the heart of the matter, which is the question of identity. He immediately addresses what is at the root of the conflict between Jesus and the Pharisees, which is the exclusivity of the kingdom of God. The nearest thing in Judaism to the kingdom of God is the rule of God on earth at the end of time, ruling over all lands and all nations.

Thus says the LORD: I will return to Zion, and will dwell in
the midst of Jerusalem. Jerusalem shall be called the faithful
city, and the mountain of the LORD of hosts shall be called
the holy mountain. (Zechariah 8:3)

They will not hurt or destroy on all my holy mountain, for
the earth will be full of the knowledge of the LORD as the
waters cover the sea. (Isaiah 11:9)

The Jews believed that only those who were born into the faith
could enter their understanding of kingdom. The Pharisees
regarded the kingdom of God, the Kingdom of Israel, as their
personal possession, belonging only to Jews under the Law of
Moses, with God dwelling within their borders. When Jesus says,
'Very truly, I tell you, no one can see the kingdom of God without
being born from above', he is using the very item that mattered
most to the Pharisees: birthright. Through this right of birth,
they excluded everyone else – such as the Samaritans, who were
'contaminated' through marrying outside the Jewish tribe and
religion. Jesus knew how sensitive this matter was to the Jews,
and he wanted them to understand that the kingdom of God is
open to all humanity, and that it is not a physical kingdom, but
a kingdom of hearts. Just look at how Paul described himself to
see how important it was for Jews to be born in the faith:

If anyone else has reason to be confident in the flesh, I have
more: circumcised on the eighth day, a member of the people
of Israel, of the tribe of Benjamin, a Hebrew born of
Hebrews; as to the law, a Pharisee; as to zeal, a persecutor
of the church; as to righteousness under the law, blameless.
(Philippians 3:4–6)

Jesus reveals very clearly to Nicodemus that what he is saying
comes from the very heart of God; he says to him that 'No one
has ascended into heaven except the one who descended from

heaven, the Son of Man' (John 3:13). He tells Nicodemus that he is revealing the truth that he experienced when he was with the Trinity, bathed in the culture of God. Taking the very essence of human culture that Nicodemus understood – birth and belonging – he turns it completely on its head, filling it with a brand-new meaning, based on the culture of God. Even today, nearly two thousand years after Jesus spoke these words, birth into a particular family brings with it certain advantages or disadvantages. Today in the Middle East, the first question you are asked concerns the identity of your father. This tells you a lot about the Middle East – it's not about education or income, it's about birth and belonging to a certain family. Birth is the beginning of a relationship; after you are born into your family, you build relationships and you grow into that culture. But, Jesus says, once you have faith you are born of the Spirit, and you then begin building your relationships accordingly. Here, he is using one of his cultural icons – family and belonging – as a vehicle to give us a glimpse of what it means to be God's family, God's tribe, God's culture!

> Jesus answered him, 'Are you a teacher of Israel, and yet you do not understand these things? Very truly, I tell you, we speak of what we know and testify to what we have seen; yet you do not receive our testimony. If I have told you about earthly things and you do not believe, how can you believe if I tell you about heavenly things?' (John 3:10–12)

Jesus is telling Nicodemus that the Sanhedrin should be experts in their own religion and its interpretation, yet they are ignorant both about Jesus' mission and identity and, more importantly, about their own faith. The religious leaders had poured all their efforts into the Law and its rigorous application on the people while ignoring the spiritual side – the relationship with God. This is how they could allow businesses to trade in the temple – they failed to consider the spirit of the Law.

Nicodemus did not expect that this conversation would reveal his ignorance about his own religion, which shocked him to the core; he wanted to engage with Jesus, and to understand his mission. The last thing Nicodemus expected was that Jesus would leave him doubting his own faith.

Just as with the woman caught in adultery – our previous example – Jesus acts as a mirror, revealing the truth to Nicodemus that it is his understanding of his own faith and mission that is questionable, not Jesus'. He repeatedly surprised everyone when he revealed the culture of God, which always surprises, shocks, transforms, provokes and inspires. Jesus did not just act as a mirror this time – he also shone the light of the culture of God directly on Nicodemus by revealing to him God's perspective on our life, faith and relationships. He made it absolutely clear to Nicodemus that God's perspective was not limited to what the Law offers. Jesus was not aggressive as he was when he met the Pharisees; he appreciated the visit, and the step that Nicodemus took to come in the night to talk to him. He admired Nicodemus, and he happily gave Nicodemus what he sought. With much love, Jesus wanted him to be liberated in his thinking, from the prison of the letter to the surprising freedom of the spirit – 'The wind blows where it chooses'. You cannot cage the Spirit in the prison of the Law!

The backbone of the whole encounter is the revelation of the culture of God. Jesus revealed that the culture of God can be known only through himself, the one who descended from heaven.

What do we learn about the culture of God in this encounter? The culture of God is:

1. Not concerned with where you are born. Jesus explained that when you are born in the flesh, you are born into a family and an earthly culture. When you are born in water and the Spirit, then you are born into God's family and the culture of God.
2. Not concerned with whether you are a religious leader or not; what is important is to understand your own faith and interpret it properly.

3. Not concerned with the letter of the Law because Jesus exceeded that: 'those who do what is true come to the light, so that it may be clearly seen that their deeds have been done in God' (John 3:21). For Nicodemus, you were judged by the Law – if you follow the Law then you are good; if you break the Law, you are evil. Jesus said that this was no longer valid. What matters is whether you embrace the light, which is Jesus himself. Many times, Christians find themselves reverting to the easy way of teaching and interpreting faith by burdening themselves with the rules and regulations of the Old Testament as well as new ones. Sometimes, we become worse than the Pharisees – look at the Puritans who banned music, theatre and dance, and today similar movements also turn the Christian faith into a book of laws. This is exactly what Jesus was against; faith is a living relationship with him, not a spread-sheet totting up rules and their violations.

Every Christian has heard, so many times, the verse that says, 'For God so loved the world that he gave his only Son, so that everyone who believes in him may not perish but may have eternal life' (John 3:16). This statement was directed to a senior teacher of the Law, breaking the whole centrality of the Law for Nicodemus. In this verse, Jesus gave Nicodemus a completely different core to faith in God. The challenge, for Nicodemus and us all today, is this: what is the heart of our faith? Is it that love which made God sacrifice his own Son, or a new rulebook? Having lived in the Levant, I understand people's desire to be guided by black-and-white rules of what to do and what not to do in their religious life. Judaism and Islam are very close in that they are focused on a divine law. Islam came into being in a desert and Islam learned from the Jewish Law and adopted from it. In the Levant, people lived under the Law of Moses, and then when Islam came it brought a similar code of laws. People in this region have been immersed in black-and-white divine laws in a way that you do not find in the West. Judaism flowered in the Levant and Islam flourished there, and both promote a strict following of divinely revealed law. Because of the influence of Islam, many Christians in the Levant tend to treat parts of the Bible as a Christian *Sharia* or divine law, especially when it comes to the Old Testament and the letters of St Paul. Here, Jesus took faith out of the destructive claws of the religious leaders and the Law and freed it to be a relationship.

The Gospel narrative continues, 'Indeed, God did not send the Son into the world to condemn the world, but in order that the world might be saved through him. Those who believe in him are not condemned; but those who do not believe are condemned already, because they have not believed in the name of the only Son of God' (John 3:17–18).

What is Jesus saying, and what is he not saying? He is not saying that all other religions are condemned. We must read this in context, in relationship to what he says before and after this. We should never think that the whole truth can be found in one sentence in the Bible! The condemnation is not to do with a certain faith or belief that is different. Jesus is highlighting the contrast between light and darkness, between good and evil, not between one faith and another. It is tempting to stop after 'Son of God' and think that we have the whole picture. If that were true, then Jesus would have stopped speaking.

'And this is the judgement, that the light has come into the world, and people loved darkness rather than light because their deeds were evil. For all who do evil hate the light and do not come to the light, so that their deeds may not be exposed. But those who do what is true come to the light, so that it may be clearly seen that their deeds have been done in God.' (John 3:19–21)

If we are in the light, we do not do evil. Jesus is saying that evil deeds belong to the people who are in the darkness, and that does not in any way mean judging people according to their beliefs. For us who believe in him, we know that, because we are in the light, then our deeds will flow from that. We are in the light because God loves us, not because we are 'good'; this is the culture of God – God loves unconditionally.

As we have seen, the culture of God is not about excluding anyone, and we shall talk about this later; the culture of God is about exposing the darkness by living in the light and reflecting it.

The Samaritan woman

Here is another perfect example of a Levantine conversation, full of imagery, allegory and metaphor, such as the water and the well. We see incredible dynamics here, as Jesus and the Samaritan woman challenge each other. It is clear that they respected each other, and Jesus rewards her for her courage and integrity by revealing his true identity to her and giving her a powerful insight into the culture of God.

> Now he had to go through Samaria. So he came to a town in Samaria called Sychar, near the plot of ground Jacob had given to his son Joseph. Jacob's well was there, and Jesus, tired as he was from the journey, sat down by the well. It was about noon.
>
> When a Samaritan woman came to draw water, Jesus said to her, 'Will you give me a drink?' (His disciples had gone into the town to buy food.)
>
> The Samaritan woman said to him, 'You are a Jew and I am a Samaritan woman. How can you ask me for a drink?' (For Jews do not associate with Samaritans.)
>
> Jesus answered her, 'If you knew the gift of God and who it is that asks you for a drink, you would have asked him and he would have given you living water.'
>
> 'Sir,' the woman said, 'you have nothing to draw with and the well is deep. Where can you get this living water?

Are you greater than our father Jacob, who gave us the well and drank from it himself, as did also his sons and his livestock?'

Jesus answered, 'Everyone who drinks this water will be thirsty again, but whoever drinks the water I give them will never thirst. Indeed, the water I give them will become in them a spring of water welling up to eternal life.'

The woman said to him, 'Sir, give me this water so that I won't get thirsty and have to keep coming here to draw water.'

He told her, 'Go, call your husband and come back.'

'I have no husband,' she replied.

Jesus said to her, 'You are right when you say you have no husband. The fact is, you have had five husbands, and the man you now have is not your husband. What you have just said is quite true.'

'Sir,' the woman said, 'I can see that you are a prophet. Our ancestors worshipped on this mountain, but you Jews claim that the place where we must worship is in Jerusalem.'

'Woman,' Jesus replied, 'believe me, a time is coming when you will worship the Father neither on this mountain nor in Jerusalem. You Samaritans worship what you do not know; we worship what we do know, for salvation is from the Jews. Yet a time is coming and has now come when the true worshippers will worship the Father in the Spirit and in truth, for they are the kind of worshippers the Father seeks. God is spirit, and his worshippers must worship in the Spirit and in truth.'

The woman said, 'I know that Messiah' (called Christ) 'is coming. When he comes, he will explain everything to us.'

Then Jesus declared, 'I, the one speaking to you – I am he.' (John 4:4–26, NIV)

Jesus did not 'have to go through Samaria'. Jews used to travel around the edges of that land because of the deep enmity between the Jews and the Samaritans. The Jews considered Samaritans unclean because they had contaminated themselves by marrying outside their faith and their tribe. In time, the religious leaders created an enormous taboo that led to the forming of a 'no-go area' around Samaria. It became normal to travel far out of the way to avoid Samaria, and to consider Samaritans as the 'enemy'.

Jesus lived deeply within his earthly culture, but he saw everything in the light of the culture of God. Because of that, he was well equipped to challenge everything that contradicted or conflicted with this culture – and the Jewish view of the Samaritans clashed greatly with the culture of God.

There is no room in the culture of God for enmity or sectarianism. The consequence was that Jesus couldn't comply with the Jewish norm of avoiding Samaria; the culture of God is the culture of love, and this love empowered Jesus to see beyond racial and religious prejudice. He saw people in Samaria who needed to experience the mercy and love of God just as much as his own people in Judaea did. Notice how the Samaritan woman acknowledged the barriers between her and Jesus, both that she was a woman and also a Samaritan: 'How is it that you, a Jew, ask a drink of me, a woman of Samaria?' She knew that Jesus was breaking a series of Jewish customs and beliefs just by talking to her.

The encounter between Jesus and the Samaritan woman powerfully summarises the meeting between the culture of God, which Jesus brought and revealed, and the religious culture that prevailed then, which was faithfully represented by the woman – a culture that was supposed to be 'God's will'! Until it is fully adopted, the culture of God will always challenge earthly religious culture, stripping it of its claims to represent God's will faithfully and accurately.

In the conversation between the Samaritan woman and Jesus, the woman was courageous enough to challenge his views, especially when she said, 'Where do you get that living water? Are you greater than our ancestor Jacob, who gave us the well, and with his sons and his flocks drank from it?' Jesus respected this challenge, and he challenged her back throughout their conversation. To explain the culture of God to the Samaritan woman, Jesus revealed himself as the Messiah, revealing that the only way to access the culture of God is through himself – as Jesus said, 'Everyone who drinks of this water will be thirsty again, but those who drink of the water that I will give them will never be thirsty. The water that I will give will become in them a spring of water gushing up to eternal life.'

No Jewish prophet, even Isaiah or Jeremiah, would have been able to make such a statement, which could only have originated in the heart of God. No prophet would have had the authority to say such things. Jesus is gradually revealing his true identity to the Samaritan woman, not only as a prophet but as the one who comes directly from God. Who would have the authority to give life, but God? By saying that he can give eternal life, Jesus is revealing that he is God. He is not a teacher, or a Pharisee, or a prophet, or even only the Messiah – he is GOD.

When the Samaritan woman says, 'Sir, I see that you are a prophet. Our ancestors worshipped on this mountain, but you say that the place where people must worship is in Jerusalem', she is acknowledging that Jesus is a prophet and she asks a typical question one would ask of a prophet. A normal prophet would have guided her in her dilemma and would have told her where the correct place to worship would be. But Jesus did not act as a typical prophet; he acted as a typical God! God always shocks us because he redirects our thinking and raises us to a completely different level of thinking. The answer was neither Jerusalem nor the mountain, nor even a third place. Jesus answers directly from the Trinity:

> 'But the hour is coming, and is now here, when the true worshippers will worship the Father in spirit and truth, for the Father seeks such as these to worship him. God is spirit, and those who worship him must worship in spirit and truth.'

What Jesus did for the Samaritan woman was to carry her with him to another level of thinking, free from the chains of 'place' and 'culture' and moving on to spirit and truth. This is just what he did with Nicodemus. Jesus challenged those he met, not by telling them that they were wrong but by inviting them to meet him in the culture of God, where everything becomes life-changingly new and clear.

The culture of God provides us with a wonderful space to meet, with no need for defensiveness or the condemnation of those who differ. This is the culture of God revealed by Jesus, and Jesus himself takes us into this culture so that we can understand his mind; this moves us beyond right and wrong to meet in Christ, moving forward together.

6

The Culture of God in the Teachings of Christ

I want to begin this chapter by talking about the importance of teachers, not just to the people of the Levant, but everywhere. Today, sadly, teachers in many parts of the world have become merely a conduit for the information required to pass exams. But teachers have often been hugely admired and respected, and at the time of Christ they were especially respected when it came to teaching the word of God.

How many of us can look back and recognise the wonderful influence of the good teachers we knew? These are the people who inspired and guided us, who opened new horizons and helped us to become all that we could be. Unfortunately, the opposite is also true. I remember very well that in two years of my school education I had very bad maths teachers; the result was that until now I have never liked mathematics and I am bad at it. However, I had successive excellent Arabic Literature teachers and they helped me to discover a gift within me, which is writing both poetry and prose. Teachers have an enormous impact; they shape minds and beliefs, they influence us and they guide us. Good teachers do not just teach the subject; they are role models for those who learn from them because they share their love of the subject.

The best teachers understand their culture and their context, teaching in an accessible way that enables their students to understand easily and genuinely. The best teachers love teaching, they love their subjects, and they love the people they teach. Sadly, teachers rarely see the fruits of their work, which may take decades or more to develop.

Jesus is a perfect example of a good teacher. He was rooted and immersed in his earthly culture and context, he loved his people, and because of that he was able to challenge them while affirming their culture and values. Jesus treated people with respect, and this respect came out of his care and love for them, especially for those who followed him. Jesus was always surrounded by crowds of people who wanted to learn from him and listen to him – what clearer proof could there be that he was a good teacher?

Jesus' teaching would have been directed at all ages, classes and levels of education. People from every walk of life would gather to hear him, and he chose the best style of teaching that would fit the vast majority of his listeners; although on occasion he taught directly, very often he told them stories, and he filled those stories not just with morality and ethics but with much about God himself and his culture. In Jesus' stories, the culture of God met the culture of the people.

In this chapter we will look at three forms that Jesus used in his teaching: parables; the 'I am' statements; and those times when he was more direct.

1. Parables

Jesus' teaching stories, which we call 'parables', were much more then moralistic tales in which the evil are punished and the good are rewarded. They contain many levels of teaching and engaged Jesus' listeners, expecting them to make an effort to understand their real significance: 'Let anyone with ears to hear listen!' (Luke 8:8). People responded to Jesus and in different ways they understood what he meant by the stories; they enjoyed the entertaining, interesting, exciting and imaginative styles that he used. The people in the Levant have always enjoyed storytelling and the proof is that Jesus' following increased dramatically. Would thousands of ordinary people have followed a man who spouted intellectual, philosophical rhetoric? When Jesus fed the five thousand, he had been teaching them beforehand. When he was as young as twelve, his teaching amazed even the teachers: 'After three days they found him in the temple, sitting among the teachers, listening to them and asking them questions. And all who heard him were amazed at his understanding and his answers' (Luke 2:46–47). All four Gospel narratives show that people followed Jesus, they listened to him and they sought his teaching. Jesus was a teacher throughout his life. The people would never have heard such teaching from their religious leaders, who would have been direct and instructive, focused on what the people should or should not do. Jesus' passionate and caring teaching style would have been so refreshing and this brought people flocking to hear him, much to the annoyance of the other teachers of the Law. It was clear from the way he taught that Jesus was not coming to establish a new 'divine law' or to abolish the old one. Instead he came to revolutionise the way people approached the Law.

The parables are open to everyone. All classes, all races, all ages and levels of education are invited to read and dig deep into them, and thereby access the culture of God, according to their level of understanding. Through these parables, the culture of God became available to everyone to explore and experience.

In order to make the parables powerful vehicles of the culture of God, Jesus used everyday images that everybody would understand – rooted in the contemporary culture, they would have resonated with the people of his time: the shepherd, the vine and branches, bread, a mother hen, a sower in a field, and so on. He wove his teachings and stories around these familiar pictures and filled them with new meaning – and by doing so, made them eternal. Every generation, in every culture around the world, can find their own way to access the culture of God within Jesus' stories.

We need to understand that Jesus' teaching was directed to the people, not to the elite and the intellectual. He had to find a way to reach these people while teaching about his original culture. How could he bring his divine thoughts to the people of the first century? He turned normal images and situations into vehicles that could carry those divine thoughts and allow the people to interpret them according to their abilities. Jesus respected the diversity of his audience, and he opened those stories for interpretation on every level – and at any time, even today. Because of that, we must acknowledge that to go deeper into the parables we need to revisit the earthly culture within which Jesus taught. By doing this, we can unpack the universal, eternal values within them. I will be returning to this in Chapter 10.

By unpacking Jesus' parables and images, we are accessing the very culture of God. Why did Jesus embed the culture of God in stories and images? Because as we dig as deep as we can into the parables to get the true treasure that lies within them, we go on our own personal journey of discovery, and the result is intimate, memorable and uniquely fitted to our own experiences. We remember what we understand and what we work out ourselves so much better than we will a dry commandment, and as we internalise the culture of God through our reading it enters deep inside us in the way that a bland statement could never do. For every generation, the parables offer fresh insight and inspiration.

In his conversation with Nicodemus, Jesus explained exactly why he taught in parables rooted in his earthly culture, 'If I have told you about earthly things and you do not believe, how can you believe if I tell you about heavenly things?' (John 3:12). This is a typical Levantine way of speaking, exaggerating Nicodemus' puzzlement; Jesus is saying to Nicodemus that if he is struggling to understand Jesus' earthly analogies and metaphors, then there is no point entering into a philosophical discussion. Jesus has to speak of earthly things first, using analogies and little stories so that his message can be understood, because he knows if he reveals the truth to people in direct language they will not understand.

The workers in the vineyard

One of Jesus' most challenging parables is that of the Workers in the Vineyard:

'For the kingdom of heaven is like a landowner who went out early in the morning to hire workers for his vineyard. He agreed to pay them a denarius for the day and sent them into his vineyard.

'About nine in the morning he went out and saw others standing in the market-place doing nothing. He told them, "You also go and work in my vineyard, and I will pay you whatever is right." So they went.

'He went out again about noon and about three in the afternoon and did the same thing. About five in the afternoon he went out and found still others standing around. He asked them, "Why have you been standing here all day long doing nothing?"

'"Because no one has hired us," they answered.

'He said to them, "You also go and work in my vineyard."

'When evening came, the owner of the vineyard said to his foreman, "Call the workers and pay them their wages, beginning with the last ones hired and going on to the first."

'The workers who were hired about five in the afternoon came and each received a denarius. So when those came who were hired first, they expected to receive more. But each one of them also received a denarius. When they received it, they began to grumble against the landowner. "These who were hired last worked only one hour," they said, "and you have made them equal to us who have borne the burden of the work and the heat of the day."

'But he answered one of them, "I am not being unfair to

you, friend. Didn't you agree to work for a denarius? Take your pay and go. I want to give the one who was hired last the same as I gave you. Don't I have the right to do what I want with my own money? Or are you envious because I am generous?"

'So the last will be first, and the first will be last.' (Matthew 20:1–16, NIV)

This parable challenges a society that is based on a legalistic lifestyle, and a legalistic understanding of faith. When any religion has a divine law at its core, the concept of 'divine justice' is very important, and it is based on a system of reward and punishment.

According to any human understanding of justice or fairness, this parable doesn't make sense and is irritating and upsetting. It goes against how the world works, and all that we have learnt about life. What was seen as divine law does not contradict basic human logic, but divine culture can go against our logic if we mistakenly understand God in terms of reward and punishment! Even today, the traditional symbol for justice is blindfolded and holding a set of scales to measure crimes and punishments, wrongs and appropriate compensation. For humans, $1 + 1 = 2$; this is why the culture of God is so exciting, and even so disturbing, because it goes far beyond human logic and our understanding of fairness and justice. God is not about divine law but about divine culture, and he does not act according to a set of rules and regulations. God is fellowship, society and culture, and out of that comes all that we understand about him and what he wants from us. If we try to understand God in terms of laws and regulations, it means we are limiting him and putting him in a box – and worse, we are saying that God wants us to live in a box. Both are wrong – God is spirit and truth! 'The wind blows where it chooses' (John 3:8a).

Looking at this parable, we see workers who are working for many hours, and each should be rewarded for the amount of time they worked. But God is looking at the hearts of the workers. The worker who begins work in the last hour would happily have accepted the offer of work earlier if it had been offered to him. We see that in the conversation. They were waiting to be hired, and as soon as they were called to work they responded eagerly! That response is very important for God, who sees us truly and rewards us for our eagerness and our willingness to work.

The contrast between the culture of God and our understanding of faith and religion is that the culture of God examines our hearts, not our actions. Our abilities differ, and God understands this.

In a system of divine law, people think that they are qualified and able to judge others because they assume they have all the tools they need in the Law. This included the misuse of the Scriptures, taking a single verse to judge others. This parable makes it so clear that God's judgement is very different from ours, and we should not try to supplant him.

In this parable, we see those who worked the full day clearly resenting those who arrived at the end of the day and still got paid. Many of us can sympathise with them. Why did they resent the latter? Because they judged that the late arrivals did not deserve their reward. The full-day workers could not look beyond a shallow understanding of fairness, and that led them to believe that they deserved more reward than the others. We see the culture of God in the vineyard owner's response, reminding everyone that he is the only judge, and his measures of fairness and justice are completely different from the workers'. We will examine this even further when we look in a later chapter at how Jesus dealt with the Law.

When we look at the Parable of the Workers in the Vineyard, the way that the owner of the vineyard treated the workers was in terms of his relationship with them, not in terms of their actions; this is how God looks at our relationships – it is an example of the culture of God. This parable especially reflects the afterlife, and the relationship between our life and our afterlife. The parable is often burdened with the misconception that the one who comes to faith at the end of his life and still receives salvation has 'won' because he enjoyed a wonderful life of earthly fun, far from God, and still made it to heaven at the last minute. But two things are erroneous here. The first is the supposition that a life of faith is a miserable life free from fun and enjoyment; the second that a change of heart on one's deathbed is a painless flick of a switch. Of course, very few of us will get detailed advanced warning of our deaths! Coming to God involves a sincere, transformational experience of changing of the heart; then, it does not matter when this happens because this change is total. As St Paul says, 'More than that, I regard everything as loss because of the surpassing value of knowing Christ Jesus my Lord. For his sake I have suffered the loss of all things, and I regard them as rubbish, in order that I may gain Christ' (Philippians 3:8).

Parables about the kingdom of heaven

He put before them another parable: 'The kingdom of heaven is like a mustard seed that someone took and sowed in his field; it is the smallest of all the seeds, but when it has grown it is the greatest of shrubs and becomes a tree, so that the birds of the air come and make nests in its branches.' (Matthew 13:31–32)

He told them another parable: 'The kingdom of heaven is like yeast that a woman took and mixed in with three measures of flour until all of it was leavened.' (Matthew 13:33)

'The kingdom of heaven is like treasure hidden in a field, which someone found and hid; then in his joy he goes and sells all that he has and buys that field.' (Matthew 13:44)

'Again, the kingdom of heaven is like a merchant in search of fine pearls; on finding one pearl of great value, he went and sold all that he had and bought it.' (Matthew 13:45–46)

'Again, the kingdom of heaven is like a net that was thrown into the sea and caught fish of every kind; when it was full, they drew it ashore, sat down, and put the good into baskets but threw out the bad.' (Matthew 13:47–48)

It is imperative, if we want to understand what Jesus meant by these parables, to understand the cultural and political environment in which he lived, as this sheds enormous light on what he said and why he chose those specific metaphors. The parables reflected the needs of the people he was teaching, and are perfect examples of the method Jesus used to reveal the culture of God using imagery and analogies from his earthly culture; he used the mustard seed, the pearl, the field and the vineyard; these became like boats carrying heavenly and godly values into the hearts of the people.

How is the kingdom of God like a net, for instance? Because it includes everyone, the 'bad' and the 'good'. God does not choose certain people to give favour to; as it says, 'so that you may be children of your Father in heaven; for he makes his sun rise on the evil and on the good, and sends rain on the righteous and on the unrighteous' (Matthew 5:45).

If we choose to be evil, we will find ourselves at odds with the culture of God, trapped in the net rather than lifted by it. The net is freedom in God rather than a prison.

In the culture of God, relationships, rather than a human understanding of justice, are most important. God looks at justice not only deeper than we do, but in a completely different way; in the culture of God, in the reign of God, the offer that God has for all human beings is beyond time and place; it is not restricted to when or where. God is focused on the sincerity of the heart's response to that call, whether it be near the beginning of life, in the midst of it, or even at its end. It is not based on what religion we adhere to. What matters is that we respond to, and embrace, the culture of God. It is the same with equality. God's understanding is very different from our own. The closest example is how a mother looks at her children and in what way she feels that they are equal. They might think that one of them is the favourite, or the least favourite, but for the mother, equality has completely different values. A mother may devote more attention to a child who is unwell or who is far away, but this does not mean that she loves that child more than the others. Equality here includes the measurement of vulnerability and need.

This book is not intended to be a commentary on the Bible, but we must look at these parables to find glimpses of the culture of God, revelations beyond human culture, imagination and thought. The people in Jesus' time were obsessed with the idea of throwing the Romans out and restoring the physical Kingdom of Israel. This obsession was spread among the people, especially by the Pharisees and religious leaders. When Jesus preached his understanding of the kingdom, it came as a shock because his interpretation of the kingdom was completely contrary to this popular belief. This contradiction was a major incentive for the Pharisees to act to silence Jesus. Ultimately, this led to the Cross and beyond.

In Arabic, a Semitic language, the word for an earthly kingdom is *mamlka* while the word that Jesus used for the kingdom of heaven is *Malakout* – one is a physical state, while the other is a reign. It is the same in both Hebrew and Aramaic.

The kingdom of God can be better understood as the reign of God. These parables are analogies, explaining some of the characteristics of the reign of God, and God's relationship with us through Christ. They reveal that this reign depends not on land or a crown but on relationships; Christ revealed that the culture of God is a culture of relationship. The culture of God is priceless, and it should be treasured and desired like the pearl or the treasure. We need to become aware of the value of the culture of God, then we shall long for it! The culture of God is contagious and unstoppable; it spreads, like the yeast, and no one can contain it. This unstoppable power is through the

Holy Spirit, as we see after the Resurrection when the disciples went from quaking in fear to going out to spread the word around the world. This is how unstoppable the culture of God can be.

The culture of God does not marginalise or destroy our human cultures. The yeast spreads in the dough, enhancing the dough without destroying it.

My mother told me that when she was young there was a tradition among Christian families in Syria to put a lump of unyeasted dough outside the house on the evening of 5 January – the night before Epiphany. In the Orthodox Church, 6 January – Epiphany – is the celebration of the Baptism of Christ rather than the arrival of the Magi. The belief is that Christ will pass in the night to bless the dough. In the morning, the Christians would bring the dough into the house, and it would now be yeasted. They would take a small part of this yeasted dough and mix it with the dough they had prepared on that day to make bread for all the family. From that day on, every day they would take a piece of the newly yeasted dough and put it aside to leaven the dough on the next day. Jesus Christ on the Cross is like the dough left out overnight, in that through the Resurrection he was brought back to leaven that generation of humanity. The disciples, carrying the faith and the experience of the Resurrection, in turn passed this through faith to the next generation. In this way, the yeast of the Resurrection keeps leavening the lives of the believers, generation after generation.

Today, we are the yeast in the world. What does that mean? First, only when we are in the world, in touch with the world, can we make an impact. Second, we need to understand that the yeast interacts with the dough; we must interact with the world, we must be active in the world, if we are to be the yeast. Third, the yeast passes its quality to the dough, and so should we; we must pass the quality of having the culture of God in us to the world through our relationships and interactions. When we share the qualities of the culture of God with others, sharing love, peace, joy and fellowship, we are acting like the yeast and those who see the culture of God in us will be transformed. Just as the yeast transforms the dough, we must transform the whole world. We can tell if the yeast was good by trying the bread; as Jesus said, 'You will know them by their fruits' (Matthew 7:16). If used properly, people taste wonderful bread – no one says, 'What yeasty bread!' Just like the yeast, we work for the world, not for ourselves.

Yeast contains within it the power to grow and to multiply. The mustard seed contains within it the potential to become a huge tree. The culture of God helps us to grow because it recognises the true potential in us and it helps us to grow by helping us to know ourselves. We need to be ready to be surprised, to expect the unexpected from ourselves when we encounter the culture of God. As Jesus said to the Samaritan woman, 'The water that I will give will become in them a spring of water gushing up to eternal life.'

The culture of God empowers us to live in our own culture abundantly and to transform that culture; the culture of God has not come to invade, to seek out and destroy other cultures. It is the culture of love, which ultimately is the final and only commandment that Jesus left for us, 'I give you a new commandment, that you love one another. Just as I have loved you, you also should love one another' (John 13:34).

Jesus taught about the kingdom of God to transform our understanding of the concept of kingdoms, giving it a completely different meaning. Jesus was not the king the people expected. He was not restoring the old Kingdom of Israel. He came to restore the kingdom of the heart, the kingdom of relationships, and this is where the culture of God works, giving us a completely new understanding of every part of life and existence.

As the world is facing religious fanaticism today in every religion, and mostly this fanaticism is based on a political ideology and agenda – even if hidden behind the mask of faith – we can see that the culture of God that was revealed in those parables of the kingdom of God stands firmly against fanatical religious ideologies. While the culture of God always affirms the good and builds relationships, it stands against evil, stripping it of its power.

Once again, we are seeing the establishment of sectarian religious states in the Levant; the Levant is trapped again in emphasising the earthly kingdom rather than the heavenly kingdom (the reign of God over the lives of the people). Humans are vulnerable to slogans and buzzwords such as 'freedom', 'independence' and 'defending the faith' that political ideologies use to influence the hearts and minds of young people. The culture of God is not about establishing sectarian kingdoms with religious police to enforce an incredibly narrow-minded outlook. Such an approach is unnatural and is destined always to fail. God is inclusive and the culture of God is for all humanity, and most definitely not for one sect or nation. Millions have been killed in the name of 'freedom' and so on, and even in the name of religion, but this has nothing to do with what God actually wants, and has always wanted, for us. Those sectarian ideologies are nothing but an abuse of the reign of God over our lives and relationships, an abuse purely for political and worldly power. In this abuse, we impose our own agenda on God to enrich ourselves, while the culture of God challenges our own agendas and helps us to explore what God wants for us.

2. Jesus' 'I am ...' statements

This is a unique style of teaching. In the Gospel according to John, we see Jesus using a different way to talk about himself, which no one else had used before. Jesus saw that he needed to explain his identity in a more direct way, using a series of metaphors to talk about himself in relationship to God and to the people. In these sayings, Jesus helped the people to understand him, directly and clearly revealing his true identity and role.

When Jesus says, in John's Gospel, that 'I am ...' he is opening the door to understanding who God is in himself and how he understands himself. This is a fantastic insight into the culture of God. Jesus used this method to differentiate himself from all teachers and prophets who had come before him, giving us a tremendous opportunity to become closer to the culture of God.

All those 'I ams' apply to God as much as to Jesus and this is why Jesus is the only gateway to enter and explore the culture of God.

Just before we look at the first example of these statements, I should point out that the Jewish name for God, Yahweh, means 'I am'. Those 'I ams' are direct identifications of Jesus with God incarnate, God in direct relationship with his creation.

I am the bread of life

Jesus said to them, 'I am the bread of life. Whoever comes to me will never be hungry, and whoever believes in me will never be thirsty.' (John 6:35)

'I am the bread of life.' (John 6:48)

'I am the living bread that came down from heaven. Whoever eats of this bread will live for ever; and the bread that I will give for the life of the world is my flesh.' (John 6:51)

In the Levant, bread is so important that it is considered holy. When I was growing up in Syria, if a piece of bread fell on the floor we would pick it up, kiss it, touch it to our foreheads and then either eat it or put it aside. We would never step on bread because it is the basic element of nourishment and a gift of God for which we should be grateful. For instance, if a piece of bread fell in the street, someone would carefully lean it against a wall so that no one would step on it. This is grace, a gift of God, and not to be abased even if it is inedible. Bread always reminds you that others will be going without.

When we break bread in the Levant, a time of great fellowship, we gather the pieces of bread together at the end of the meal and put them back in the bread basket or bag for later consumption. Please remember that we tear our bread to eat, so none of the pieces would have bite marks!

Bread is an essential item that no home should be without, as well as a major symbol for social bonding; breaking bread with someone means that you are bonded. There is a saying in the Levant when two people have broken bread together: 'Between us we have bread and salt.'

Notice that Jesus does not say that he is 'like the bread'. He made it clear that he and the bread are one and the same. At the Last Supper, Jesus did not say when he broke the bread that 'This IS LIKE my body.' He said, 'This IS my body.'

When Jesus picked the metaphor of bread to talk about himself, he was totally aware of the depth of that metaphor, as well as its many meanings in his earthly culture. He knew that his body would be broken, just like we break bread. Jesus presented himself as the most basic nourishment of life; even if you have nothing else, bread can sustain you. When two or three are gathered in Jesus' name, he is the bond that joins them together, a role that bread also fulfils. All this would have been understood by the people of the Levant. Bread was prepared and baked at home, so everyone knew how to bake it. Every home would smell of newly baked bread – the most welcoming smell in human experience. When you visit a home which has Jesus at its centre, the metaphorical fragrance of his presence cannot be missed.

Jesus associates bread with life itself. He is the basis of our lives, the nourishment we need, and the bond in our families and communities. Jesus is life itself.

Jesus knew that people would associate this bread with their nation's experience in the wilderness centuries before, when God provided them with manna – bread – from heaven. The message is clear: he is the one we need, and the only one. How does this metaphor reveal the culture of God? It reveals that the culture of God is a culture of community that bonds with love, as Jesus gave himself out of love. The culture of God is the culture of giving, of gathering, of sharing, bonding, and life itself. This culture is life-giving, the culture of life itself. Christ speaks out of his experience of his original culture, when he was with the Father, bonded with the Spirit of Love. In the same way, we are bonded with Love, not with the Law – which is all the religious leaders were offering!

I am the true vine + *You are branches.*

'I am the true vine, and my Father is the vine-grower. He removes every branch in me that bears no fruit. Every branch that bears fruit he prunes to make it bear more fruit. You have already been cleansed by the word that I have spoken to you. Abide in me as I abide in you. Just as the branch cannot bear fruit by itself unless it abides in the vine, neither can you unless you abide in me. I am the vine, you are the branches. Those who abide in me and I in them bear much fruit, because apart from me you can do nothing.' (John 15:1–5)

In the Mediterranean region where I come from, we have a lot of vineyards, especially in the mountains near Lattakia. I grew up visiting the town of Kassab where my uncle's family had a vineyard and a field of apple and olive trees. There, I experienced for myself how my uncle used to look after the vines and how he removed the branches that were not fruitful. The vine is a unique plant, which is neither a tree nor a bush; it has a stem, which is not very thick, and the branches grow on a horizontal net two metres above the ground. The branches climb the net and spread out along it.

I used to see how my uncle would exercise quite a ruthless method of removing the branches that were not bearing fruit. These branches obstruct the growth of the tree and use up precious resources in the soil. This process of cutting the dry branches happens alongside another harsh process, which is pruning; cutting healthy branches to guide the growth of the plant and encourage new growth. I used to ask my uncle why he was cutting healthy branches as well as dry and dead ones, and he would smile and say, 'I remove all of each dead branch, but I only cut off a calculated part of a healthy branch in order to make it grow even better.' Even after it is pruned, the healthy branch remains firmly attached to the stem and it still receives nourishment.

Sometimes, when we feel pain and we go through troubled times, we may feel that we have been severed from the vine and left to wither. We need to remind ourselves that as long as we are connected to the culture of God, the culture of love, this feeling of isolation and abandonment is the product of our situation but it is not a reflection of reality. Through the risen Christ, we are forever connected to the vine, which is God and the culture of God.

When Jesus talks of 'abiding', he is talking about being rooted and strongly connected. St John often uses 'abiding', especially when he speaks about love – 'God is love, and those who abide in love abide in God, and God abides in them' (1 John 4:16). The best way to remind ourselves of this connection to the vine and to the culture of God, even in the middle of the darkest times in our lives, is to keep a line open, through prayers, with the living Lord. This lifeline, this open line, can be for shouting, screaming and even expressing anger to God. This is what it means to abide: all our relationships have ups and downs; so does our relationship with God. That does not mean that we love him less or he loves us less.

The culture of God gives us the best model of how we should interact with each other and with God. Even Jesus felt that he was abandoned ('My God, my God, why have you forsaken me?' Matthew 27:46b), but that did not make him any less the Son of God, and it did not make God love him less. This has always been my message to Christians, especially those in the Levant, who have so often felt severed from the Body of Christ and even from the love of God. I feel that I want to scream at them, and say, 'I felt this before, and God is with us in this dark time.' Jesus' promise is true. When we keep abiding in him, and he in us, nothing can cut us off. As St Paul said in his second letter to the Corinthians:

> We are afflicted in every way, but not crushed; perplexed, but not driven to despair; persecuted, but not forsaken; struck down, but not destroyed; always carrying in the body the death of Jesus, so that the life of Jesus may also be made visible in our bodies. (2 Corinthians 4:8–10)

3. Direct teaching by Jesus

We have already seen how Jesus taught through parables, and how he used metaphors to explain his identity and purpose. Jesus was a teacher, and on occasions he taught his people directly. The difference between Jesus and the other religious leaders in his time was profound, because he saw that the religious leaders' teachings did not help people come closer to God; he saw that their teaching was designed to make the people totally dependent on them and their instruction because their teaching focused on the burdens of the Law. Those teachers did not help anyone to build a living, loving relationship with God, and he experienced and knew how far those leaders and their teachings fell from the culture of God that he experienced first-hand. Jesus could not ignore that the leaders were leading the people astray, taking them further from God rather than closer to him.

But Jesus was not trying to work against the faith and the religious identity of his people. Instead, what he resisted was the way that the religious leaders interpreted religion to gain and wield worldly power. Throughout his life, from birth to Ascension, we see this collision between the leadership of Jesus Christ and the religious leadership of his time, because he always wanted the people to live their faith with joy and to experience God's love as they practised their religion. The Pharisees and the scribes only focused on putting chains of rules and regulations on the people, paralysing them and preventing them from experiencing this fruitful and beautiful, dynamic, living relationship with the Creator God.

Therefore, instead of only clashing with the religious leaders and entering into debates with them, Jesus turned directly to his people and taught them how he believed their relationship with God should be. He taught them not only through parables and metaphors, but in a direct and revolutionary way that corrected the religious leaders' teachings. The best example, which gloriously reflects the culture of God, is what we call the Sermon on the Mount, which we find in the Gospel according to Matthew, and the Sermon on the Plain in the Gospel according to Luke.

The so-called Sermon on the Mount is a true diamond, multi-faceted and endlessly compressed! There is absolutely no way anyone could discover everything that this diamond holds in its heart. This direct teaching of Christ is a revolutionary response to the religious leaders' abuse of the Law. The question is: how did Jesus deal in essence with the Law, revealing the culture of God? His method was a direct and bold comparison between what was said to the people before (what was handed on to them in the Old Testament) and what he himself teaches. Jesus says, 'You have heard that it was said … But I say to you …' He also used other phrases, such as 'You have heard that it was said to those of ancient times … But I say to you …' It is amazing that he did not say, 'God told you … But I say to you …' At no point does he associate those laws with any divine power – he only puts it in a passive form: 'You have heard'. Jesus is now giving a deeper, higher principle than the old ways of 'do' and 'do not do'. In this contrast, Jesus is telling us bluntly what God thinks about those issues, and this is in itself the culture of God. Jesus did not abolish the Law. He fulfilled it, taking it to a higher level, liberating people from a long list of imperative orders so that we can, each one as best we are able, grow in the knowledge of the culture of God. This is a completely different worldview from the limiting worldview that the Law used to offer.

We all know that everybody is equal under the Law, as they are in civil law, which means that the Law should be applied to everybody in exactly the same way. Jesus does not believe that there should be a divine law like this. Why? Because Jesus believes and knows that we are not equal; we are all different. We are different in our abilities, whether that is to pray, to fast, to give, to love, to forgive and so on.

Simply, Jesus acknowledges in the deepest sense the diversity in our abilities and our relationships with God. Let's look at an example of Jesus' words as he compares what had been said with what he said: 'You have heard that it was said, "You shall not commit adultery." But I say to you that everyone who looks at a woman with lust has already committed adultery with her in his heart' (Matthew 5:27–28).

In the Ten Commandments, there is the direct order: 'You shall not commit adultery.' Adultery in this context is simply sexual intercourse with another man's wife – and that man had to be Jewish. What did Jesus then teach about adultery that was different? He involved another commandment, which is: 'You shall not covet your neighbour's house; you shall not covet your neighbour's wife, or male or female slave, or ox, or donkey, or anything that belongs to your neighbour' (Exodus 20:17). In this commandment, wives were considered property 'that belongs to your neighbour', in the same class as houses, slaves and beasts of burden. In this teaching, Jesus lifts these two commandments, combining them into a high principle, directed to men, prohibiting them from even 'looking at a woman with lust'. This means every woman, all equal in value, and he is widening the act of adultery from being an actual sexual act to how we consider women, how we see them. 'Don't consider women as property' is a much higher principle than

'Don't have sex with your neighbour's wife', and it is more difficult, a call for us to strive to live up to that standard. This is the culture of God, which is not based on reward and punishment but on building human relationships as God intends us to do.

Jesus took the basics of the Law, which is an egalitarian principle of 'to do or not to do', and turned them into high principles that all of us can strive to reach according to our own abilities. In the teachings of Jesus, we see the Law evolving into a kind of relationship with God into which we are all invited, respecting our differences in building that relationship. This is far removed from the 'tripwires' of the Law, which measured us only on whether we did something 'naughty' or not. Now, we are to be measured by how much we do with what God has given us. The new challenge is not to fall foul of the Law but to raise ourselves ever higher, endeavouring to reach the immensely high standards that Jesus himself set.

'Ask, and it will be given to you; search, and you will find; knock, and the door will be opened for you. For everyone who asks receives, and everyone who searches finds, and for everyone who knocks, the door will be opened' (Matthew 7:7–8 and Luke 11:9–10).

This is a style of life that Jesus is promoting for us to follow. It is a life that is proactive, dynamic and filled with activity that builds good relationships with God and with each other. The culture of God is dynamic and giving, and we are unable to know it if we are passive; only by asking, searching and knocking can we live in it. There is no way to know and live the culture of God without searching for it; it demands action. When Jesus asks us to live this style of life, he does so because he wants us to grow, and to strive to be better.

This style of teaching reveals that God intentionally created us different from each other. It is not an accident, but God's purpose. Because we are different, and made that way by God, the ways we build our relationships will all be different. Some of us are more intellectual than others, some are more emotional, or more passionate, or more charming. Our ways, perspectives and methods for building relationships are as unique as our fingerprints. When it comes to relating to God, some will be more spiritual, others more legalistic, some will fear God, some will treat him as a friend. God loves each one of us and he respects the individual way that each of us has in how we build our relationships with him. God is diverse himself, within the Trinity. In the culture of God, in the way that Jesus respected the many ways that people related to him and in the way he communicated with the people, we see that God knows that we cannot all obtain the same relationship with him. God gives himself to all of us, and he loves us equally.

Jesus is revealing through this perspective on the Law that faith is not about what to do and what not to do; it is about a living and breathing relationship with God who knows our shortcomings and limitations, and loves us equally and desires this relationship with us, however weak or strong our faith is. What matters to God is that we do our best!

> 'And whenever you fast, do not look dismal, like the hypocrites, for they disfigure their faces so as to show others that they are fasting. Truly I tell you, they have received their reward. But when you fast, put oil on your head and wash your face, so that your fasting may be seen not by others but by your Father who is in secret; and your Father who sees in secret will reward you.' (Matthew 6:16–18)

Here Jesus tackles a very sensitive religious practice, which is part of the Law: fasting. Since fasting can easily be an invisible practice that would not be noticed by others, people tended to make a show of it in order to show how religious they were and how strenuously they followed their faith. Every religion suffers from the abuse of this practice because many people try to impose their fasting on others by trying to look either tired or irritable to give themselves an opportunity to reveal that they are devoutly following this religious practice. Jesus hits out at hypocrites because most religious practices should be undertaken without a public show of piety, as the aim of those practices is to become closer to God rather than to garner praise from others. If ever we seek reward for our religious devotions, then at least let God reward us, not other people. Faith is not self-promotion, showing off how 'good' we are. It is the ability to build a living, constructive relationship with God and with each other. Again, Jesus here strongly dismisses any interpretation of faith or religion in terms of reward and punishment, putting the whole evaluation of our faith in the hands of God alone.

When Jesus said, 'Do not judge, so that you may not be judged. For with the judgement you make you will be judged, and the measure you give will be the measure you get' (Matthew 7:1–2), what he is saying is so profound. He is saying that what you sow you shall reap. The judgement of God is a judgement of love, not condemnation. God is love. God is not there to judge you, but to help you to love others and to turn your judgement into love. God is waiting for us to call upon him to fill our measures with love; then 'The measure you give' will be filled with love, as will be 'the measure you get'. The less we judge, the better able we are to love, and the more we love, the less we judge. Consequently, the closer we are to God, to Love, the more we are able to let judgement go and to grow out of the habit of judging people. Jesus said, 'I judge no one' (John 8:15) because he loves everyone. St Paul says that 'There is therefore now no condemnation for those who are in Christ Jesus' (Romans 8:1). This is the culture of God.

> '... and if anyone wants to sue you and take your coat, give your cloak as well; and if anyone forces you to go one mile, go also the second mile. Give to everyone who begs from you, and do not refuse anyone who wants to borrow from you.' (Matthew 5:40–42)

Jesus talks about giving your cloak as well as your coat, and about going the extra mile. What is the principle that Jesus is teaching here? First of all, he is transforming that part of the Law that seeks an eye for an eye into an absolute principle that touches the essence of the relationship between God and humanity, which is generosity. I spoke before about the importance of generosity to the people of the Levant, and Jesus is teasing this principle, giving it an infinite depth plus a divine quality which cannot be understood or accepted by our human cultures. This is the culture of God. What Jesus is saying is that there should be no limit to our generosity; we are all called to live in an unlimited expression of generosity according to our different abilities.

Such a speech could easily be seen in any human culture as stupid or weak, especially when it comes to turning the other cheek. Jesus was not stupid. He understood the difficulty of such teaching in any human culture, and especially at that time when people were ruled by the heavy hand of rules and regulations in the name of God. Jesus had to share this teaching with us, because he had experienced the beauty and the joy of living those principles in his original culture, and he wanted to share with us a glimpse of the inner life of God.

Jesus wants us to understand that we should not treat God as someone who needs to be pleased by rituals and offerings.

> 'So when you are offering your gift at the altar, if you remember that your brother or sister has something against you, leave your gift there before the altar and go; first be reconciled to your brother or sister, and then come and offer your gift.' (Matthew 5:23–24)

Here, Jesus is saying that God does not need physical presents and gifts; what he wants from you is a gift of a clean heart. If God looks into your heart and sees anger or hate, then no amount of gifts would be enough to please him. A statement like this from Jesus shows us why he never in the whole of the New Testament talked about 'religion' in the sense of institutions and buildings. He spoke about a living faith and a strong, free relationship with God rather than building temples and creating rituals. In the whole of the New Testament, at no time do we hear of Jesus going into the temple to make an offering or sacrifices; Jesus is the sacrifice himself.

When Jesus was teaching these deep principles, he did and does not expect us to fully implement them. Jesus did not come to give us a new set of laws, especially such a difficult set of 'laws' to follow! He lifted the burden of the Law by giving us the freedom of trying to live to his principles as much as we can. Jesus wants us to try to turn the other cheek; he knows that we fail sometimes, and he respects that because he was human and he experienced weakness himself.

It is very important that we are careful not to turn Jesus' teachings into laws and burden each other with them, and not to see any failing as a sign that we are 'not Christian'. We are not meant to turn these principles into laws and judge each other according to them or to try to implement them as laws ourselves; we will *always* fail, and it would become a self-defeating faith. We are called to try our best, to learn from them and to strive to reach them with the awareness that we never will do so. Because we are trying, we are firmly connected to the culture of God.

This multi-faceted diamond, the Sermon on the Mount, is a magnificent teaching that transforms everything we know about faith and religion into a powerful force that can aid us on our journey with God, and to God. Jesus did not give us teachings that were impossible to follow, but rather guidelines on how to build a relationship with God. He reveals that belonging to the culture of God, and being citizens of his kingdom, means to continuously work on improving and growing in that relationship with him.

How do we do that? We do it exactly in the way that we build a friendship with another person. We must get to know them better, because we love them and we desire this friendship. The better we know them and love them, the more we seek to strengthen the communication with them. With God, getting to know him through Christ requires us to read and study the Scriptures, just as Jesus did. We see in all his teachings how immersed he was in the Scriptures.

Also, the way of communication with God is prayer. There are two levels to prayer, and the first is talking to God. Here I do not mean kneeling beside our beds and saying a prayer we memorised when we were children, or even worse by turning God into a shopping service that we present with a list of our needs! Prayer is a state of being constantly with God. It is the ongoing awareness that God is with us, and we are with him every day, every minute. We make that happen, in the beginning, by consciously praying or talking with God in our hearts and minds at different times of the day no matter what we are doing, even to dedicate a minute to talking with God while we are walking in the street. The more we do that, the more it becomes part of our existence and our daily routine; it becomes second nature. The second level is that communication also means being aware that God talks to us – it is not a monologue but a dialogue. The culture of God is a dialogue within the Trinity, and we see that Jesus was in a constant dialogue with the Father throughout his life. We need to listen carefully and observe how God communicates with us through, for example, other people, through the Scriptures, and through occurrences in our lives. God does not stop talking to us through everyday life, and we must be open to those messages from God. This is not paranoia, but a heart-warming exercise where we invite God every day to be the centre of our lives.

We also build our relationship with God by observing our relationships with other people, and examining from time to time whether those relationships are built on the principles of his culture rather than selfishness or the trend of the day. Finally, the relationship with the living God should be manifested in our own growth in our faith and in furthering our spiritual journey. That does not mean that suddenly all problems in our life will disappear. What it means is that, when we have problems, we know that we are not alone in facing them; God is with us.

7

The Cast of Characters: the Culture of God in Relationships

One of the best books that explores the people around Jesus and how they looked at this extraordinary personality is, for me, *Jesus the Son of Man*, written by the great Lebanese author Gibran Kahlil Gibran (1883–1931). I remember very well reading this book again and again, beginning when I was a teenager. What fascinated me was the psychological journey that Gibran embarked on, as he wrote about the major characters who surrounded Christ in his short ministry. As I was developing the concept of the culture of God, I remembered this great author who grew up in the Levant and then emigrated to the United States, where he wrote many of his books, including *The Prophet*. He managed to remain faithful to his roots in the Levant while he wrote in English for a Western audience; the result was a book that reveals the inner soul of the people who lived with the Master, Jesus Christ, during his life and ministry.

When God decided to take the risky step of the Incarnation and became a human being, he chose one of the most diverse and vibrant communities in the world. This was a place where so many cultures met: the militaristic Roman Empire, the intellectual and cultured Greeks, the devoutly religious Hebrews, and the native Assyrians. It was a place where many other cultures came for trade, for pilgrimage and even for tourism. As the Acts of the Apostles tells us in the story of the first Pentecost, Jerusalem was host to people from all over the known world – in fact, by the first century AD, the Silk Road reached from the Pacific Ocean, through India and modern-day China, all the way to Damascus, Tyre and Alexandria. The people around Jesus reflected this diversity. We have different circles that were in touch with the Master himself. We have his family, then his disciples; we also have his close friends like Lazarus and Lazarus' sisters Mary and Martha. Then there are his followers and disciples who were not part of the inner circle, as well as the people who came to him to learn, to ask questions or to be healed.

We need to understand how Jesus interacted with all of these people if we are to see how God himself understands social interaction and relationships.

How Jesus chose his disciples

The reason I am exploring the relationship of Jesus with his disciples is that Jesus revealed so much of the culture of God within those relationships, from which we learn much of the qualities of God. Look at his answer to his disciple Philip, when Philip said, 'Lord, show us the Father, and we will be satisfied' (John 14:8).

Jesus answered:

'Jesus said to him, 'Have I been with you all this time, Philip, and you still do not know me? Whoever has seen me has seen the Father. How can you say, "Show us the Father"? Do you not believe that I am in the Father and the Father is in me? The words that I say to you I do not speak on my own; but the Father who dwells in me does his works. Believe me that I am in the Father and the Father is in me; but if you do not, then believe me because of the works themselves. Very truly, I tell you, the one who believes in me will also do the works that I do and, in fact, will do greater works than these, because I am going to the Father. I will do whatever you ask in my name, so that the Father may be

glorified in the Son. If in my name you ask me for anything,
I will do it.' (John 14:9–14)

Jesus says that everything in their relationships reveals the Father:
everything he is sharing with the disciples, teaching them, building
friendship – all this interaction reveals the culture of God. This
is the best opportunity for us to gain access to how the Father,
through the Son, is dealing with humanity. This is the culture of
God: when we explore Jesus' relationship with his disciples, we
are seeing how God himself would have built those relations.

Looking at the way Jesus called his disciples, we can describe
it as sometimes extremely unusual, sometimes puzzling and on
occasion absolutely shocking – especially for the Levant in the
first century. Intellectual and spiritual 'Masters' usually choose
the best and the most intelligent students to whom they can pass
on their message. They become the bearers of the Master's torch
and they need the ability to understand and preach the message
to the world. Jesus went against the current and shocked everyone
by the nature of the people he chose. Today, we can take his
choices too much for granted: 'Of course he chose simple fishermen to carry the message from God …' We do not think of
the cultural implications of his choices. We must realise that in
the eyes of the rabbis and the people Jesus must have appeared
to be crazy. Jesus chose his disciples very deliberately, although
he could have attracted the best, the richest and the most intellectual and educated in his society.

Look at *Matthew*, who was a tax-collector. Don't imagine him
to be a civil servant in the pay of the authorities. He would
literally have had to win an auction in order to get that job,
because it was very profitable and thus much sought after. To
get the income, you would need to put pressure on the people,
treating them mercilessly to squeeze the highest possible 'taxes'
out of them. In addition, the tax-collectors lent money at high
interest and they were despised for collaborating with the occu-
pying Roman powers. Jesus should have stayed away from a man

like Matthew, but instead he went directly to him and called him by name, asking Matthew to follow him. I am sure that Matthew would have been totally shocked by Jesus' call; he must have been amazed that he was chosen as a disciple by a teacher and prophet who was already getting to be noticed and respected. Matthew would have known a lot about Jesus – part of his job was to know about everyone and everything in his province, including the gossip and the rumours, as he needed to know who was prospering, who was getting money and who was losing it. Matthew would have had informers, his 'eyes and ears' in every part of society. We take it for granted that Matthew gave up everything and followed Jesus; we should realise how much he gave up, and the huge risk he took by following Jesus and giving up his income and the power that had always protected him from the wrath of the people. Matthew had to give up everything; all he had left was his discipleship. Jesus also risked his own reputation when he called such a man into his inner circle.

Where is the culture of God here? Simply put, God thinks differently! This is the mind that transcends our way of thinking. Jesus did not choose Matthew because of his abilities, but because he wanted to show the glory of God's power working in Matthew's life and just what Matthew could do when he allowed God to work in him. What merely human mind would have worked in this way?

Another of the disciples, *Peter* – a middle-aged and poorly educated fisherman – is a very different example of Jesus' astonishing choice. His face and his hands would have been burned by the sun, his hands were rough and calloused, and he would have stunk of fish. This was a man who had wrestled with the sea, who had faced storms and dangers, who would have lost friends to the deep. He had nothing to do with the temple, with theological debates or interpretations of the Law. He could not have made a 'speech' of two words even in front of five fishermen, but he would have known the power of command when he sailed his own boat. He must have heard about Jesus through community gossip and through his brother Andrew, who was a follower of John the Baptist, but he would not have been very interested in Jesus. Jesus and Peter would have had almost nothing in common.

Peter reminds me a lot of my own life, growing up by the Mediterranean Sea in the Syrian port of Lattakia. There, I often watched fishermen weaving their nets and preparing to go to sea; sometimes they would leave in the morning and return in the evening, while others would be gone for days. I can still hear them singing as they wove their nets. The fishermen would land their boats and take their catch to the fish market, which was near my home, stopping on the way to buy ice from the ice factory, before putting out their fish to sell on beds of broken ice. Those men lived a very challenging and difficult life, just as Peter must have done. Their personalities had been shaped by the sea, the waves, the rocks and the storms. We can see the effects of a life at sea on Peter, who was incredibly passionate, impulsive, stormy and unstable but loyal and loving.

Although I did not like fishing myself, my father was a very keen angler and my older brother, my cousin and my brother-in-law were all ship's captains. Life at sea was a big part of how I grew up; my nickname was the 'Son of the Sea'. The sea has had its effect on me as I am passionate and stormy too. Because of this, Peter feels like a member of my family!

Jesus took this raw material and revealed glimpses of his original culture through Peter and his tempestuous personality. The unstable, ever-changing, passionate Peter was called the exact opposite by Jesus – 'The Rock'. The rock can be something stable and a solid foundation – but at the same time ships can break apart on a rock. Because of that, it's a matter of navigation and how you approach the rock. Jesus knew how to approach Peter. Through him, Jesus taught the disciples and the Church through the ages how to turn our faith into a stable and firm basis for our relationships.

Let's look at an incident to see how Jesus revealed a fantastic glimpse of the culture of God through Peter. This incident also happened to take place at sea.

> When evening came, he was there alone, but by this time the boat, battered by the waves, was far from the land, for the wind was against them. And early in the morning he came walking towards them on the lake. But when the disciples saw him walking on the lake, they were terrified, saying, 'It is a ghost!' And they cried out in fear. But immediately Jesus spoke to them and said, 'Take heart, it is I; do not be afraid.'
>
> Peter answered him, 'Lord, if it is you, command me to come to you on the water.' He said, 'Come.' So Peter got out of the boat, started walking on the water, and came towards Jesus. But when he noticed the strong wind, he became frightened, and beginning to sink, he cried out, 'Lord, save me!' Jesus immediately reached out his hand and caught him, saying to him, 'You of little faith, why did you doubt?' When they got into the boat, the wind ceased. And those in the boat worshipped him, saying, 'Truly you are the Son of God.' (Matthew 14:23b–33)

Matthew tells us this extraordinary story, of when the disciples were tortured by the wind and the waves in the middle of the Sea of Galilee – also known as the Lake of Gennesaret. They had spent a terrifying night in the midst of a storm that threatened to destroy their boat. Just before dawn, Jesus himself appeared to them, walking on the very surface of the lake. As so often was the case, he was waiting to see their reaction. As he probably well expected, the disciples' hearts were full of fear and disbelief to the extent that they thought he was a ghost. In their young faith, they could not imagine that what they saw would be Jesus in the flesh. Hearing their cries of fear in the storm-tossed sea, and seeing how exhausted they were from fighting the storm all night, Jesus reacted in his typical way to reassure them and give their hearts some peace. That peace would eclipse their fear and the power of the storm.

The bold, uncompromising Peter decided to test the floating apparition and said to him, 'Lord, if it is you, command me to come to you on the water.' Peter being Peter, he was so taken by what he saw and by his love of the Lord that he did not only test the apparition – he included himself in a real test of faith.

Breathtakingly, this also shows that Peter knew that, if it was Jesus, then he would have the authority to give that order. The problem started when Jesus did so – it was now up to Peter to prove his faith. Did Peter actually think that Jesus would say 'yes'? If he did, then he was prepared to risk everything, even his life, to obey the Lord and to fulfil his word. The simple fact that Peter stepped out of the boat showed that he already exceeded the faith of the vast majority of us even at our absolute best and most faithful. Knowing the anger of the sea myself, I could imagine the total shock of the other disciples in the boat as Peter began to clamber over the side. I am sure that they thought he had lost his mind, even if it was Jesus himself who had commanded him. No one else, however, spoke to the Lord or tried to stop Peter, showing that they were paralysed by fear.

Before we continue looking at this amazing encounter, I want briefly to talk about that storm. I remember once, when I was on my brother's ship in the middle of the Mediterranean Sea, he called me to come to the bridge. Although it was night and I was tired, I went to the bridge. I looked through the windows and I saw a huge storm surrounding us. When the lightning coursed through the pitch-black sky, it was like veins of light running through the darkness of the clouds. I was terrified. My brother said to me, 'Watch the wave.' A huge wave came straight towards us. I thought we were dead; but the wave broke harmlessly on the bow of the ship and the seawater cascaded across the deck. When I think of Peter in his little open boat, I shiver and remember the storm I witnessed in the safety of a modern vessel with satellite navigation. I thought of Peter, and I said to my brother then that just to have the thought of stepping out of the boat would have been total madness! I would not have stepped out of the bridge, let alone off the ship and into the sea. My brother told me that he had not wanted me to miss a storm at sea because it is unlike anything you can experience on land. As the captain of the ship, he was not afraid; he was calm and content, doing his job. This life-changing cataclysm was normal for him. Although Peter was a captain of a vessel like my brother, and he would have seen many storms, this would not have prepared him for Jesus' command to leave the boat and walk upon the sea!

Peter was much more courageous than I would have been, although I do not know what would have happened if Jesus himself had commanded me to step off the ship and face the Mediterranean at that moment.

'So Peter got out of the boat, started walking on the water, and came towards Jesus.' Peter, looking at Jesus, did indeed step on the water and started walking. Although his few steps towards Jesus proved to Peter that it was the Lord, the nature of the sailor kicked in and a lifetime's experience with the sea made him look at the storm; with that, he lost his focus on Jesus. Once he started looking at the storm, the storm distracted him and he was unable to concentrate on the presence of Jesus, and at that moment he began to sink ...

Let's leave Peter now, and look at the incident from Jesus' position. Jesus saw that the disciples were fighting the waves. He could have silenced the storm at any time – as he did at another time when he was in the boat with the disciples and he calmed the storm – but instead he decided to engage with them on a different level. He wanted to see how they would react to him when he came to them in their time of distress. Would they see him as a refuge or would he add to their fear and confusion? By coming to them across the waves, Jesus revealed himself to be the polar opposite of the storm. How would the disciples handle the two opposites?

Jesus did not calm the storm as he approached them. The storm was a source of fear and destruction while Jesus' presence was one of peace and life, and he placed himself as the opposite of the storm as he responded to the disciples' cry of doubt.

I imagine that the Lord would have been delighted by Peter's reaction! Peter did not just want to test the figure on the water – he wanted to test himself too. Through that test, Peter wanted to demonstrate to himself and to the other disciples that Jesus is indeed the opposite force to the storm. I can picture a smile of love and encouragement appearing on the Lord's face as he saw Peter climb out of the boat. Perhaps there was even a little admiration. Peter actually left the boat!

Inevitably, after a couple of steps, Peter started to sink. 'Lord, save me!' Peter's cry is proof that he actually believed that this was Jesus standing before him. Those seconds that Peter spent on the water were sufficient for him to direct the cry for help to Jesus rather than his friends in the boat. Jesus had made the whole encounter an opportunity to reveal a glimpse of the heart of the culture of God. We see that God cannot be but in the centre of our lives and our existence, and once we lose that focus we allow the storms around us to swallow us. As long as we keep our eyes and our attention on the Lord we can go through the storms with peace in our hearts. As long as we are centred in God, then we live in his magnetic field, drawn to that centre, which helps us to go through life with faith and hope and love. This incident should remind us of Jesus saying, 'I am the vine, you are the branches' (John 15:5). As long as the branch is joined to the vine then the branch will be strong and it will flourish. Our strength and our nourishment come from the vine. But once the branch is separated from the vine, it withers. Once Peter looked at the storm, he separated himself from Jesus and the power of the storm nearly overwhelmed him – for that moment, Peter was severed from the power that he could have drawn from

Jesus. However, Jesus is completely anchored and drawn into the Father at all times through the Holy Spirit.

We cannot talk about Jesus and his disciples without stopping at the very special relationship that bonded Jesus with *John*. What kind of relationship did John and Jesus have, and how can we understand it from two perspectives: the culture of their time, and the culture of God?

Having lived my childhood and youth in the Levant, and having lived in Europe and the West now for over twenty-five years, I can see very clearly the difference between the Levant and the West in terms of personal relationships, especially deep friendships between men. In the Levant, a man's life would not be right if he did not have a special close male friend. Such a friendship is vitally important for any man in that region. In the West, closeness between men is almost exclusively restricted to school, but very rarely beyond that. Let me elaborate and talk about a concept that is very differently understood in the West. This concept is intimacy.

In the West, the word 'intimacy' indicates the absence of barriers but mostly it encompasses sexual relations. In the Levant, intimacy means closeness, total trust, deep sharing and fellowship, and a sense of being soul mates. All my time in the Levant, I experienced, deeply and beautifully, such intimacy in friendships. My intimate male friends played a major role in shaping my personality and my thoughts. They helped me to open up my heart and mind unreservedly to another human being who would also open his heart and mind to me without any agenda. Levantine men can never share their thoughts and feelings with their wives and female friends in the way they can with their closest male friends. Culturally, the kind of fellowship that men have with each other is very different from the fellowship when women are there, or the relationship between a man and a woman. This is a fact of life in the Levant, and in this culture even the language is different between men. Levantine men, from the time of Jesus until today, are not afraid to be physical with each other; I remember I used to go to school with my intimate friend arm in arm every day. Even teenagers and adult men would walk hand in hand or arm in arm, or with our arms round each other's shoulders. This type of physical contact has no sexual connotation whatsoever. Sometimes, it makes me very uncomfortable that every physical contact between men in the West is avoided because men do not want to hint at any sexual connotation. In the Levant, we speak with our hands and bodies; so it is normal for me to touch another man's knee, hand or arm when I am talking to him.

This is very important if we are to explore the very special friendship between Jesus and John. That friendship can easily be described from the Levantine perspective as 'intimate'. It is obvious from the Scriptures that Jesus and John were intimately close; and John accompanied Jesus even to the Cross. The person written about as 'the disciple that Jesus loved' in John's Gospel is probably John referring to himself (though many scholars think this is simply an unknown, unnamed disciple). Whoever he was, one of the disciples laid his head on Jesus' chest during the Last Supper; as odd as this may sound to many in the West, this would have been normal between intimate friends in the Levant.

It is John who made the most courageous revelation in the history of humanity, saying directly who God is when he said in his first Epistle (1 John 4:16): 'So we have known and believe the love that God has for us. God is love, and those who abide in love abide in God, and God abides in them.' What does John mean by 'love'? John deliberately uses a paradoxical language when he says that 'God is love'. It is nonsensical in any language to make anyone the synonym of a concept, such as 'This judge is justice.' You could say that the judge was just, or that he acts justly; but he or she cannot 'be justice'. The aim of John here is to say that love and God are interchangeable. The very essence of God is love, and love is not only an attribute of God. We can only speak in a human way, and every language has different words for, and meanings of, 'love'. In Greek, there are four words,

greek –
Love =

philia, agape, storge and *eros*. *Philia* is friendship, a strong regard between equals. *Eros* is sensual or sexual love. *Storge* is the love of parents for their children. Finally, we reach *agape*; charitable love, the unconditional love of God for his children. Thomas Aquinas described *agape* as 'to will the good of another'. Not every language has such distinctions. In Arabic, there are only two words for love and they share a common root; *mahaba* means general love, while *hob* means romantic love – and general love as well! In Arabic, there is only one verb *to love*. I believe that John's meaning of love transcends all languages and categorisations. The love of God is a holistic, inclusive self-giving which we are unable in any language fully to define. The best we can do is to immerse ourselves in understanding how God shows his love to us.

Here, in this intimate, special relationship with John, Jesus is teaching us that intimacy belongs to love, which is at the heart and the essence of the Trinity, and the content of the culture of God.

We have John to thank that we see this vulnerable side of Jesus and just how he did not shy away from intimacy and closeness to other human beings. Love makes us vulnerable because we are exposed to the possibility of being hurt and our defences are low. This is the nature of love, that when we love we open ourselves to the other and trust them. On the Cross, we see that humanity's evil took advantage of the absolute love that God showed in Jesus Christ and we attacked God in killing the innocent Jesus.

How he interacted with those in need

Love is the only perspective that Jesus used to deal with people; he believed that love does not only give people what they need, but also challenges and transforms them. The love that Jesus practised shows us the kind of love that the Trinity enjoys.

How did I come to this conclusion? All kinds of people, from the poorest and the most marginalised to the richest and the most powerful, approached Jesus for different reasons. One group of people that Jesus met with sympathy and tender love was those in need, whether it was physical, emotional or spiritual. He always found the time, the energy and the wisdom to respond to those needs in an inspirational way that often transformed their very lives. He also made those vulnerable people channels of God's love for others, using their own needs to address problems shared by the whole community. Let's look at a profound example: the woman who suffered for twelve years with haemorrhages (Matthew 9:20–22, Mark 5:25–34, and Luke 8:43–48).

Now there was a woman who had been suffering from haemorrhages for twelve years; and though she had spent all she had on physicians, no one could cure her. She came up behind him and touched the fringe of his clothes, and immediately her haemorrhage stopped. Then Jesus asked, 'Who touched me?' When all denied it, Peter said, 'Master, the crowds surround you and press in on you.' But Jesus said, 'Someone touched me; for I noticed that power had gone out from me.' When the woman saw that she could not remain hidden, she came trembling; and falling down before him, she declared in the presence of all the people why she had touched him, and how she had been immediately healed. He said to her, 'Daughter, your faith has made you well; go in peace.' (Luke 8:43–48)

According to the Jewish Law, during their period women were unclean because of the blood they shed. Let's imagine ourselves in the place of this sick woman. For twelve years she was unclean and, because of this, couldn't touch or be touched by anyone. What are the further implications of this for her? For twelve years she had been barred from the temple, forbidden to practise her faith. For twelve years she had been unable to be a wife or a mother, or a sister or a neighbour. As long as she bled she had to be isolated and shunned. Anyone who touched her would become unclean also. For twelve years she was a source of disgust, socially rejected, isolated and marginalised. This woman was a symbol of how cruel a community could be in the name of religion. In the Levant, for an individual to suffer like this is especially devastating because life in the Levant is deeply social. Separated from the community, she was deprived of the social network that could bring her respect, joy and dignity as well as that safety net that every community forms to protect and support its members.

This woman, severed by the Law from the entire community and even from God himself, was despairing and utterly desperate. The Scriptures tell us that she had tried every means to become healthy and regain her place in her community, but she had failed.

I remember when I lived as a child in Lattakia that one of our neighbours was a disabled black man, the first black person that we had ever seen. As children, we were terrified of him; every time he appeared at the end of our alleyway, all the neighbourhood children would scream and flee in terror! We always hid from him. Even the adults ignored him. They did not know what to do with him. Understandably, this poor man felt isolated, rejected and marginalised, and he did not know what to do to be accepted by the community and by the children. The only person he could approach was my father, because he was a policeman. The poor man asked him if he had done anything wrong, and he asked for his help. My father understood the depths of this man's agony because of the importance of social relationships in our culture. I was the youngest in my family, so my father started with me, explaining that this man was just like us, a good person, and only his skin colour was different. Then he took me to meet him. I was apprehensive, but I wasn't afraid because my father was with me. The black man talked to me gently and I saw that there was no reason for me to run away from him just because he looked different. My father asked me to talk to the other children, and I did. Over time, we stopped running away, with the support of some of the adults in our alleyway. At last this man could feel welcome and at ease in our community.

In the Levantine culture, hospitality and generosity are right at its heart; this poor woman, much like the black man in my story, could not give or receive hospitality or generosity from those around her. We know from the story that she had heard that Jesus was coming to her neighbourhood, and the talk of the community meant that she would have known who he was. But he was a man and she was a woman, and interaction between them in public was forbidden. Also, she was aware that everyone knew that she was unclean and she could never approach him. What could she do? She could not lose this opportunity, but she could not embarrass herself or Jesus in front of the crowd. She must have thought that if Jesus was all that she had heard about him, a great and extraordinarily powerful healer from God, then it would surely be enough just to touch the edge of his cloak as he passed by. Her plan was to keep herself hidden, and do this and disappear; she could then see what happened. By no means did she want a scene in front of everyone, even if she were healed.

Now let's look at the encounter from Jesus' perspective. Here he is, walking with his disciples amid the crowd, with people asking him questions or asking for favours, curious to meet this famous man they had all heard about. Jesus was aware that there was great interest in him. Suddenly he felt that someone in the crowd purposely touched his cloak, and for him it was as if they were the only two people in the street. The faith of this woman was so powerful that it caught his heart and captured his attention. He couldn't take another step. When he stopped and asked, 'Who touched me?', he did not do so because he didn't know. He stopped because he wanted *everybody* to know. There would have been, I am sure, some Pharisees in the crowd who were observing every move and every little detail.

Jesus stopped and said, 'Who touched me?' The crowd was silent ... has somebody done something wrong? Peter, often impulsive, rebuked Jesus because he was surprised that he would ask such a silly question. 'Master, the crowds surround you and press in on you.' Many people must have touched him. Remember that touching was not a taboo in the Levant, it was normal.

Jesus being Jesus, he explained to Peter and to everybody why he asked that question. He specifically described a special touch that took power out of him – not just a casual bump in the street. The woman was cornered by Jesus' determination to 'out' her. She thought her touch was so discreet, yet she realised that she would have to own up and be shamed. She was trembling with fear.

Jesus meant to make a scandal out of this. But why would he be so harsh? He wanted to make the healing of this woman a public announcement of the work of the love of God over against the religious persecution of this woman because of her illness. He turned this event and this woman into a channel of transformation and challenge to the woman and to the whole community that had shunned her. We also know that, according to the Law, you needed to show yourself in public and for a priest to declare that you were healed and no longer unclean. Making this a scandal, Jesus played the role of a priest and he restored this woman, giving her back her place in the community, in the temple and in her family. He not only healed her and gave her the joy of being clean again, he also – as usual – restored her troubled heart and filled it with his peace.

What does this amazing encounter tell us about the culture of God? That the Trinity is a community of peace and generous hospitality, which has the power to heal, to restore and to rebuild what religion has corrupted. The culture of God goes beyond 'religion' and laws because it is from the culture of the heart that an eternal water of peace and mercy springs. It responds to and connects with a living faith. The healing of this woman is a beacon of hope and reassurance that God is himself a relational being who seeks to connect with us and to build a relationship of love with us.

Another powerful example that sheds light on how God thinks

concerning what is best for us – which often goes beyond our own understanding – is the healing of the paralysed man in Capernaum (Matthew 9:1–8, Mark 2:1–12 and Luke 5:17–26).

> When he returned to Capernaum after some days, it was reported that he was at home. So many gathered around that there was no longer room for them, not even in front of the door; and he was speaking the word to them. Then some people came, bringing to him a paralysed man, carried by four of them. And when they could not bring him to Jesus because of the crowd, they removed the roof above him; and after having dug through it, they let down the mat on which the paralytic lay. When Jesus saw their faith, he said to the paralytic, 'Son, your sins are forgiven.' Now some of the scribes were sitting there, questioning in their hearts, 'Why does this fellow speak in this way? It is blasphemy! Who can forgive sins but God alone?' At once Jesus perceived in his spirit that they were discussing these questions among themselves; and he said to them, 'Why do you raise such questions in your hearts? Which is easier, to say to the paralytic, "Your sins are forgiven", or to say, "Stand up and take your mat and walk"? But so that you may know that the Son of Man has authority on earth to forgive sins' – he said to the paralytic – 'I say to you, stand up, take your mat and go to your home.' And he stood up, and immediately took the mat and went out before all of them; so that they were all amazed and glorified God, saying, 'We have never seen anything like this!' (Mark 2:1–12)

This story is often used by theologians and biblical scholars to point out the divinity of Christ: that Jesus was indeed God in human form (a proof of the Incarnation). Only God forgives sins, and so Jesus' forgiveness of sins infuriated the religious leaders, because in this way he was claiming the powers of God and the authority to act in this way. The dangerous thing for the

Pharisees is that even the people knew that the forgiveness of sins belongs only to God. To them, Jesus seemed to be making himself equal to God; either he was, therefore, a blasphemer or he really was divine. It also demonstrates very clearly the quality of social relationships in the Levant at the time. Here we have a small community, probably of family, friends and neighbours, who heard that Jesus was visiting a house in town. Knowing about Jesus and his works, they thought immediately of the disabled man who lived among them. They acted quickly and thought that, if they could carry the man to Jesus, he could receive healing. As any Levantine community would do, the healthy strong men came together and carried the disabled man all the way to where Jesus was staying. They arrived there and found that the house was full inside and outside, and most probably they found other sick people there who had come with the hope of being healed. One typical scenario that I can picture is that the closest person to the disabled man would have gone to Jesus' host and explained their great need. The host would have expressed sympathy, but he would have been unable to make a way for the paralysed man to get to Jesus because of all the sick people already waiting. The man's relatives and friends, looking around in desperation, asked the host if they could remove part of the roof, which was probably a terrace roof made of straw and wooden beams, so that they could lower the man from the roof to Jesus. Remember that this is a small community, where everyone knows everybody; do not picture a big, impersonal city where all are strangers. I believe that the host, seeing their passion, would have given his permission to them. And so the paralysed man was lifted onto the roof and lowered down by his friends and relatives.

Let's now look at Jesus and imagine how he would have observed what was happening. I am sure that he noticed the roof being lifted away above his own head while he was teaching and talking to the crowd. I think Jesus would have been amused, and very curious as the hole above him got bigger and bigger. What are they up to? As he was preaching, he would have seen this paralysed man being lowered in front of him on a stretcher. He would have loved the whole scene, and the love and the care of the friends and family of that poor man. He would have seen their faith in the efforts they had made, and he would have been deeply touched by this act of ingenuity. Jesus also knew what kind of crowd was around him; that some of the crowd came to be healed, others came to listen to his wisdom, and also present were the Pharisees who came to catch him if he said or did anything against the Law.

Jesus did not just tell the man to get up and walk, which he could have done so easily; this is what the people expected. He chose instead to show the whole crowd how God would react to such a situation. He turned to the man and said, 'Son, your sins are forgiven.' I believe that such a statement had a very different impact on the different people around Jesus. It might have been disappointing for the disabled man and his family and friends because they were, understandably, hoping for a physical healing. They would have been surprised to hear what Jesus said. Not even priests had the authority to forgive sins; they could only ask God for forgiveness. The family did not know the depth of Jesus' statement and its true meaning, which is that the culture of God is caring and forgiving, and that Jesus had the authority to think and act as God does. The others in the crowd would also have been surprised and a little disappointed.

The true target of Jesus' statement were the teachers of the Law who were skulking around, waiting for him to slip up. Here they thought they had him! His statement would have appalled the self-righteousness Pharisees. Who does this man think he is? Forgiving sins? Even we cannot forgive sins! Jesus would have sensed their anger and resentment; he knew how provocative and inflammatory his pronouncement was, because he was aware that forgiveness of sins belongs exclusively to God and that no human being could do this.

In the past many people considered sickness to be a punishment from God, so it was seen as an indication that God was angry with you if you were sick. Jesus is saying that sickness and disability belong to life, and he reveals the priority that God values, which is your heart first, then your body. Jesus used this encounter to show us the culture of God: how God thinks about us, and how our healing starts from inside, not outside; the healing of the soul, rather than the healing of the body. By forgiving the paralysed man's sins, Jesus turned the priorities of religion and faith upside down by acknowledging the man's humanity, which was in greater need of healing than his broken body: like that man, we all need forgiveness of our sins. He was telling us that, for God, the heart is what is important. As he said in the Sermon on the Mount, 'If your right eye causes you to sin, tear it out and throw it away' (Matthew 5:29). He is focused entirely on the heart rather than on physical perfection. He reset the priorities with a single statement: all of the Law, obsessed with physical wellbeing and ritual cleanliness, was superseded by what really matters for God, which is the heart and the soul. Who is a better person: a physically healthy man with a dark heart, or a disabled man with a pure heart? Jesus is saying that our hearts are much more important that the superficial, ritualistic ideas of 'cleanliness' and sacrifices. Even today, there is an increasing obsession with beauty and youth.

Jesus said to the Pharisees,

'Why do you raise such questions in your hearts? Which is easier, to say, "Your sins are forgiven you," or to say, "Stand up and walk"? But so that you may know that the Son of Man has authority on earth to forgive sins', and then he turned to the paralysed man and said, 'I say to you, stand up and take your bed and go to your home.' (Luke 5:22b-24)

Jesus' answer has two parts: first, he asks which is easier – forgiving sins or telling a paralysed man to get up and walk? In asking this, he shows God's priorities – that the heart is more important. And second, in the act of healing the man, Jesus reveals his true identity as God incarnate, to the shock, astonishment and fury of the Pharisees. What could they do, though? Jesus commanded the man to get up and walk – and he did. This demonstrated, even to the Pharisees, that Jesus meant what he said when he forgave the man's sins: he did have authority!

Jesus could have pleased everybody by telling the man to get up and walk in the first place, but if he had done so he would not have taught us God's priority. His way of teaching was never just to please or to garner popularity, but to show us the culture of God. The whole event was one of the rare times in the life of Christ where he boldly, directly and unapologetically revealed his divine identity. It was as if he was saying, 'If you still don't get it, this is who I am!' Jesus was a teacher, and he preferred to live with the people as one of them, not to separate himself as a scary Divine Lawgiver – which is why this very direct episode was a rare one.

By forgiving sins, Jesus showed us, clearly and sharply, that God had indeed decided to come and be one of us. This shows that in the heart of the culture of God lay God's decision to engage directly with humanity to reconcile the world to himself. Jesus had been touched by the faith of the people who had brought the disabled man to him, and he responded compassionately. What is interesting here is that he responded not to the faith of the paralysed man but to the faith of those around him. We learn nothing about the paralysed man; in none of the Gospel accounts does he say or do anything (with the exception of Luke's account where, after he is healed, he 'glorifies God'). This teaches us something else about the culture of God: the heart of God accepts acts of faith on behalf of others whom we see to be in need. This is a significant lesson about the culture of God and its engagement with our faith and even our culture. This is why we pray for each other out of love and concern and care. Believers are one community, the members of which share their concerns and lift each other to God.

How Jesus interacted with those he wanted to challenge

Jesus put himself on a collision course with the Pharisees because, for him, forgiveness of sins, mercy and reconciliation with God were at the very heart of religion, while the Pharisees burdened their people with the minutiae of ritual cleanliness and endless rules and sacrifices. Jesus offers the culture of God – mercy, liberation and compassion – to us all, and it speaks to our hearts and souls rather than concerning itself with outward cleanliness and the things of religion.

One example of this revolutionary message is when Jesus was invited to Simon the Pharisee's home for a meal (Luke 7:36–49).

One of the Pharisees asked Jesus to eat with him, and he went into the Pharisee's house and took his place at the table. And a woman in the city, who was a sinner, having learned that he was eating in the Pharisee's house, brought an alabaster jar of ointment. She stood behind him at his feet, weeping, and began to bathe his feet with her tears and to dry them with her hair. Then she continued kissing his feet and anointing them with the ointment. Now when the Pharisee who had invited him saw it, he said to himself, 'If this man were a prophet, he would have known who and what kind of woman this is who is touching him – that she is a sinner.' Jesus spoke up and said to him, 'Simon, I have something to say to you.' 'Teacher,' he replied, 'speak.' 'A certain creditor had two debtors; one owed five hundred denarii, and the other fifty. When they could not pay, he cancelled the debts for both of them. Now which of them will love him more?' Simon answered, 'I suppose the one for whom he cancelled the greater debt.' And Jesus said to him, 'You have judged rightly.' Then turning towards the woman, he said to Simon, 'Do you see this woman? I entered your house; you gave me no water for my feet, but she has bathed my feet with her tears and dried them with her hair. You gave me no kiss, but from the time I came in she has not stopped kissing my feet. You did not anoint my head with oil, but she has anointed my feet with ointment. Therefore, I tell you, her sins, which were many, have been forgiven; hence she has shown great love. But the one to whom little is forgiven, loves little.' Then he said to her, 'Your sins are forgiven.' But those who were at the table with him began to say among themselves, 'Who is this who even forgives sins?'

The shocking thing about this story is that Simon invited Jesus to his home in order to show him that he thought he was Jesus' superior; he meant to degrade and offend him. If we know anything about Levantine culture, we know that it could never be an accident for an invited guest to be treated so offensively with such a clear and ostentatious display of a lack of hospitality. Jesus later confronts Simon about his disgraceful behaviour, after he has been further provoked by Simon himself – at the beginning of the story, we see that Jesus says nothing about his mistreatment. He had arrived, as invited, for a meal, and his host had performed none of the common and basic courtesies of hospitality expected at that time. One of them would be to bring water so that your guest could wash the dust of the road from their feet. Even now in the Levant, you greet your guest with a kiss on the cheek to make them feel welcome. To show even more hospitality, you would at that time have anointed their head with oil. In the Levant, olive oil has been considered holy for millennia, and the basis of life in the region. If you had nothing to offer your guest, you would at least be able to offer them bread and oil. Psalm 23:5 gives us a glimpse both of these cultural norms and of how God himself shows us hospitality: 'You prepare a table before me in the presence of my enemies; you anoint my head with oil; my cup overflows.'

This Pharisee, a cultured man, did none of these – yet Jesus said nothing and sat down to eat. Simon would have invited many people to come to this meal so that he could show off – the famous teacher was visiting him! – but also show everyone that he could offend him with impunity. This was a power game.

In the Levant, homes are open to everyone. Growing up in Lattakia I remember many times that our home was open for guests and I understand completely, coming from that environment, how Simon would have opened his doors wide and filled his house with people – especially as he was a leader of his community. In that atmosphere, it would not have been difficult for a stranger – the 'woman in the city' – to enter, to be welcomed and to be offered food. Simon would have known of her, this woman 'who was a sinner', and knowing what she was, he would have seen this as a rare opportunity to test Jesus. How will Jesus react to her presence?

What the woman then did to Jesus was definitely culturally unacceptable. Women would never approach men, let alone let their hair down in public. In the Levant, then and now, a woman's hair is considered special; there is a saying that 'the hair of a woman is her crown'. I remember some Orthodox priests would not give Communion to women who had not covered their hair. So, for this woman to dry a man's feet with her hair was degrading and disgraceful. One step after another, her actions became more and more humiliating for her and for those who were present – with the exception of Jesus. She then kissed his feet, the ultimate humiliation for her. The other guests at the meal would have been very embarrassed, and they must have been waiting for Simon to intervene. Why was he doing nothing?

Simon was watching and waiting for Jesus to react. This was not the behaviour of a host; he should have intervened to end this deeply embarrassing situation and shield his guests from this intruder. 'Now when the Pharisee who had invited him saw it, he said to himself, "If this man were a prophet, he would have known who and what kind of woman this is who is touching him – that she is a sinner."'

Simon clearly did not know Jesus, who could never be embarrassed by such a ploy.

Notice that Jesus did not react to the woman; he reacted to the thoughts of Simon's heart. He knew exactly how Simon was thinking, and that Simon had set out to embarrass and insult him. Jesus, the teacher, calmly and peacefully turned to Simon and told him a little story that included a profound question: 'A certain creditor had two debtors; one owed five hundred denarii, and the other fifty. When they could not pay, he cancelled the debts for both of them. Now which of them will love him more?'

Let's look at this little parable. In it, the creditor is God, and the only obvious interpretation is that we, as broken human beings, are the debtors, the sinners. The story has two elements: the element of forgiveness, and the element of love. What does it mean when Jesus says, 'When they could not pay, he cancelled the debts for both of them'? Both debtors were in trouble because they could not pay. We are all in trouble because we have all fallen short of what God expects of us and his commandment of love. Just like the debtors, we cannot clear our own debts and we need our failings to be forgiven. This is what Jesus has shown us, again and again: mercy, love and forgiveness. We saw in the story of the paralysed man that forgiveness had a connection to faith; Jesus reacted to the faith of the people who brought the man and forgave him his sins. Now, in this parable, forgiveness has a direct link to love. Forgiveness should fill the hearts of those who are forgiven with gratitude and love for God, because only God forgives sins. Logically, from this parable we can see that the more God forgives us, the more we love him. The result of forgiveness is liberation and the more we are forgiven the more we are freed from the chains of sin (anything that separates us from the love of, and the culture of, God) and remorse.

Simon could not escape the logic of Jesus' very obvious question. 'I suppose the one for whom he cancelled the greater debt,' Simon answered. Jesus affirmed Simon the Pharisee's wise answer.

Simon knew that his own plans had backfired a little. He did not know that there was much more to come!

Jesus turned to the woman, acknowledging her presence, and indirectly indicated that the parable was about her. 'Do you see this woman?' What a cheeky question – he was asking Simon, in other words, 'Are you aware that such a sinner is in your home?' Without waiting for an answer, Jesus began to demolish Simon by comparing him unfavourably to the very woman he detested in his heart.

Jesus listed all the ways that Simon had failed to demonstrate hospitality to his guest, in contrast to how the woman had treated him. Jesus highlighted that every single thing that Simon had not done, the woman had done instead – and more!

'I entered your house; you gave me no water for my feet, but she has bathed my feet with her tears and dried them with her hair. You gave me no kiss, but from the time I came in she has not stopped kissing my feet. You did not anoint my head with oil, but she has anointed my feet with ointment.'

With this comparison Jesus turned everything upside down. Simon was instantly transformed from the proud host into the disgraced person, and the woman who was supposed to be disgraced according to social norm, became the hospitable host and the hero. Jesus forgave her sins and lifted her up as an example of courage and love. It reminds me of what Jesus said to his disciples: 'for all who exalt themselves will be humbled, but all who humble themselves will be exalted' (Luke 18:14b).

This is an incredible story, connecting the love of God and his reconciliation through the forgiveness of our sins. Forgiveness and reconciliation work hand in hand, and both require willing hearts. The Pharisee showed hospitality but his heart was not willing. Although the woman's behaviour was, culturally speaking, outrageous, Jesus saw her heart was good and so she was forgiven and reconciled.

Jesus again unveils his divine identity and shows us that his teachings and interactions with the people around him reflect nothing less than the very culture of God – a culture that is centred around love and self-giving. Jesus made himself a mirror to Simon, exactly as he had done when he confronted the Pharisees who brought him the woman caught in adultery. Simon looked at Jesus and saw the ugliness in his own heart and the deformed nature of the religion that he had devoted his life to guarding. Simon also saw in the mirror of Jesus that being a man of God does not mean arrogantly judging others and using them for your own ends. The culture of God that Jesus shows us here is transformative and thought-provoking because we all become Simon at points in our lives. It is immensely difficult for any human being, especially a religious leader, to take this woman's role, to decide consciously to deny ourselves and empty ourselves in this way. It takes a lot of faith and love, and a very strong will.

If we look at this woman, we can see how she put her self-worth at Jesus' feet. Through her humiliating actions, she shed her dignity and made herself worthless in the eyes of those around her because all that mattered was to show Jesus honour. Just as this woman humbled herself before everyone, God himself humbled himself by coming to us, becoming one of us, and facing our evil on the Cross. God himself had taken the free decision to play the role of this woman to all humanity. This is a glimpse of the inner life of the Father, the Son and the Holy Spirit. The Father gave us the Son through the Incarnation, through the mud and the dirt of being a human being. This incident should remind us of when Jesus humbled himself and washed the feet of the disciples, and how disturbed Peter was by this (John 13:1–15). God in Christ, through this act of washing their feet, was washing all our feet – in the Levant, the feet are symbolically the dirtiest part of the body. The image is God shedding his dignity and his worth at our feet. The thought might sound horrifying to us, but it reveals the depth of the culture of God and just how far love can go in serving the beloved. It displays nothing less than the ultimate image of the Servant King.

The Pharisees, in their attempts to silence Jesus, actually provided him with many opportunities to touch the lives of the people in the way that God wanted. Jesus presented to his society a striking contrast between the religion that the religious leaders were promoting and the reality of God's expectations for their relationships with him. The more the Pharisees resented Jesus and fought against his way of teaching, the more love and compassion Jesus released. We see many instances of this when the Pharisees criticised him: for example, concerning healing on the Sabbath. For the Jewish leaders, the Sabbath was one of the religious themes on which they could impose their authority. They turned God's commandment for his people to rest and focus on him on the Sabbath into a confusing legal minefield of 'what to do' and 'what not to do'. Through this, the people depended on the Pharisees for guidance as to what was permissible on the Sabbath. It reminds me of the fatwa kiosks that opened in the Metro stations in Cairo to provide people with the right religious pronouncements about every little details of their lives. They put imams in those kiosks and people queued to ask those imams about everything from the great matters of life to the most mundane. It is the same mentality, reminding the people that they cannot live without the religious leaders or else they will risk God's wrath.

An excellent example is a single Sabbath day when Jesus clashed with the Pharisees twice as to the meaning of the Sabbath itself and who has the authority to define that concept.

Early on in the Gospel accounts, the Pharisees complained to Jesus that his disciples were eating the heads of grain in a field on the Sabbath day.

One sabbath he was going through the cornfields; and as they made their way his disciples began to pluck heads of grain. The Pharisees said to him, 'Look, why are they doing what is not lawful on the sabbath?' And he said to them, 'Have you never read what David did when he and his companions were hungry and in need of food? He entered the house of God, when Abiathar was high priest, and ate the bread of the Presence, which it is not lawful for any but the priests to eat, and he gave some to his companions.' Then he said to them, 'The sabbath was made for humankind, and not humankind for the sabbath; so the Son of Man is lord even of the sabbath.' (Mark 2:23–28)

According to the Law, reaping was forbidden on the Sabbath, and this included removing any part of a plant from its source of growth. Jesus' first response was to remind the Pharisees of their famous king; the Jews always boasted that they were the sons of David. King David broke the Sabbath on a much bigger scale than the disciples by eating the special bread in the temple that was reserved only for the priests. Again and again, we see how Jesus silenced the religious leaders of his time who constantly tried to trap him and to put up obstacles to stop the people coming closer to God without their permission.

This time, Jesus went much further to make a scandalous declaration by crowning himself the Lord of the Sabbath. This explosive statement in front of the Pharisees revealed that he was no less than God himself. How could the Pharisees let Jesus live when they heard him time after time identifying himself with God, and making himself and God interchangeable? Jesus was a huge threat to them. We will explore this more when we talk about the Cross and the culture of God.

Later on the same Sabbath day, Jesus healed a man who had a withered hand.

Again he entered the synagogue, and a man was there who had a withered hand. They watched him to see whether he would cure him on the sabbath, so that they might accuse him. And he said to the man who had the withered hand, 'Come forward.' Then he said to them, 'Is it lawful to do good or to do harm on the sabbath, to save life or to kill?'

But they were silent. He looked around at them with anger; he was grieved at their hardness of heart and said to the man, 'Stretch out your hand.' He stretched it out, and his hand was restored. The Pharisees went out and immediately conspired with the Herodians against him, how to destroy him. (Mark 3:1–6)

The condition of this man was not life-threatening, so healing him would be a violation of the rules of the Sabbath. Jesus was very aware of this. We need to remember that those religious leaders were putting such rules and regulations in the name of God as a way to define the people's relationship with him. According to those rules and regulations, people were supposed to measure whether they pleased or angered God. The mood of God was to be decided by how faithfully and diligently they applied the Law as interpreted by the Pharisees.

As usual, the religious leaders were observing Jesus very closely, especially on the Sabbath. Jesus, in his revolutionary way, asked the man with the withered hand to come forward, and then asked the relevant question, which would concern God rather than religion or the Law: 'Is it lawful to do good or to do harm on the sabbath, to save life or to kill?' The essence of the question is: can you do good on the Sabbath even if it is considered work and therefore forbidden? This question deals with the relationship between the culture of God and our cultures, because, according to the religious culture spread by the Pharisees, any kind of 'work', as set out in the thirty-nine definitions they had written, would be 'wrong'. In contrast, the culture of God comes from God's heart, which is good; doing anything good means that we are taking part in God's culture. This simple yet deep question silenced the Pharisees and it shows how shallow their understanding of God was and how much their leadership was based on power rather than listening to what God really wants to share with us. In this, Jesus was exercising a completely new model of leadership.

These examples of how Jesus handled one of the most sensitive issues in religious life at that time shook the thrones of the religious leaders and put their authority into question. Observing the Sabbath was the most visible religious practice that could be easily judged and controlled by the leaders at that time. It could also be exploited to control the people, so when Jesus challenged this he challenged the Pharisees' very authority. It was not easy for the entire leadership system to observe this man, the son of a carpenter, becoming a force that could bring down the might of the Sanhedrin, the Council of the Pharisees.

Jesus' new model of leadership was one of leadership through service, which came directly from the culture of God. Jesus showed us, through his compassion and his service to his people and community, that the culture of the Trinity is a self-giving one. God the Father, Son and Holy Spirit is the God of empowerment rather than oppression and punishment. Jesus always emphasised that through the Incarnation, by God becoming human, God wanted us to see and understand that his culture is a culture of care and love, far from the picture that many of the religious leaders painted, which was an image of an angry, warlike and vengeful God. God does not seek to try us and punish us.

Although he readily criticised leaders for abusing their position, Jesus never rejected or spoke against the existence of organised government or religious bodies. For example, he never attacked the structure or existence of the Sanhedrin; rather, he attacked the heavy hand of some of the members of the Sanhedrin on the people's lives. His purpose was not to destroy the Law and the religious structure that supported it; he came to 'fulfil' the Law – which means bringing it to fruition in himself so that we do not need to follow the Law of Moses – and to reform the religious structure so that it would help the people rather than control them. The people had become dependent on the religious leaders, and the role of the latter was no longer empowering or supporting – it had become authoritative and controlling. Sadly, we see that even in the Church today. Any organisation can fall into the trap of serving itself rather than serving the people.

Dealing with women

Many of Jesus' most interesting and provocative encounters were with women. Although women in the Levant have not always been oppressed by a male-dominated society, they most certainly were in Judaea and the surrounding states at the time of Christ, especially by the male religious leadership.

As we have seen, Jesus stood up for the woman caught in adultery and the haemorrhaging woman. He saved both from being destroyed by the religious system and social customs. There would have been female disciples around Jesus, although they were not part of his inner circle of twelve, who followed him and listened to his teachings. They would have played an active role in his ministry. In Luke 8:1b–3, we read that 'The twelve were with him, as well as some women who had been cured of evil spirits and infirmities: Mary, called Magdalene, from whom seven demons had gone out, and Joanna, the wife of Herod's steward Chuza, and Susanna, and many others, who provided for them out of their resources.'

I have chosen two out of Jesus' many encounters with women to see how these, in particular, allowed Jesus to give us a special insight into the culture of God. The first is with the Syro-Phoenician, or Canaanite, woman. The women of much of the Levant today could still accurately be described as Syro-Phoenician!

The Syro-Phoenician woman

This incident occurred when Jesus decided to get away from the pressures of his daily life around Galilee, and travelled to the cities of Tyre and Sidon in modern-day Lebanon. At that time, this coast was still known as Phoenicia, after the ancient civilisation, and to the Romans it was part of their province of Syria

– as indeed was Galilee. Jesus wanted some quiet time with his disciples. But his fame had preceded him.

The story of Jesus' meeting with the Syro-Phoenician woman must have existed as an oral tradition before the writings of Matthew and Mark. People in the first century rarely had access to the written word, and so it was usual to memorise stories and quotations. This encounter must have been particularly powerful as it left a deep impression on the disciples that they would never forget.

> Jesus left that place and went away to the district of Tyre and Sidon. Just then a Canaanite woman from that region came out and started shouting, 'Have mercy on me, Lord, Son of David; my daughter is tormented by a demon.' But he did not answer her at all. And his disciples came and urged him, saying, 'Send her away, for she keeps shouting after us.' He answered, 'I was sent only to the lost sheep of the house of Israel.' But she came and knelt before him, saying, 'Lord, help me.' He answered, 'It is not fair to take the children's food and throw it to the dogs.' She said, 'Yes, Lord, yet even the dogs eat the crumbs that fall from their masters' table.' Then Jesus answered her, 'Woman, great is your faith! Let it be done for you as you wish.' And her daughter was healed instantly. (Matthew 15:21–28)

In this profound story of an incredible encounter with an extraordinary woman, we need to look at what happened from three different perspectives. We start from the perspective of the woman. Here is a mother, desperate, with a wounded heart, devastated to see her child sick and tormented. As a mother, she would be ready to do anything to help her sick child. She hears about this teacher and miracle-worker and she sees in him perhaps her last hope for curing her daughter. She comes to him with determination and passion, throwing herself at his feet, begging for help, and she would not leave without his aid. She was fully aware that she came from a different religious background. But her focus was on her mission and her mission was to save her sick child. Nothing was going to stop her from this and she was ready to break every barrier, of religion, culture and gender, to do this. She did not listen to the disciples moaning about her, she would not give in to those no doubt trying to push her away. She clung on to her hope, even though she would have been deeply hurt by the way the disciples treated her.

Now let's look at how the disciples saw the scene. They were far too aware that they were in the Gentiles' territory, which meant 'outsiders' and those who did not belong to 'the faith'. They looked down on the Gentiles, especially through the lens of ritual uncleanliness, and they felt superior to them. Of course, 'they were better than the people here'. This woman was bothering them, screaming for Jesus, and she would not let go. Since they had failed to send her away, because of her fixation on Jesus, they turned to him and asked him to 'Send her away, for she keeps shouting after us.' In addition, it was considered 'wrong' for a woman to approach a man in this way, so the disciples' reaction was typical of their culture. They did not shy away from displaying their dismay at the woman's persistence. Why would Jesus not make her leave? Jesus' holy silence would have been filled with a lot of noise by the unhappy disciples.

How did Jesus himself see the whole scene, and what did he make of what was unfolding around him? He closely observed both 'sides' in this story. On the one hand, he was listening to the desperate cry of the mother, feeling her pain, moved to help; on the other hand, he heard the shouts of his restless and irritated disciples who wanted him to send her away. From the whole story, I can imagine Jesus growing angry with the disciples' attitude, and taking his time to formulate a lesson that they would never forget. This story shows us in one incident the two sides of Jesus: the one who is a meek and mild, sympathetic healer, and the tough teacher who went an extra mile, if needed, to teach the right lesson – especially to his own disciples.

It might appear that Jesus' first response was to ignore the woman. But silence does not always imply indifference. As in the story of the woman taken in adultery, when Jesus bent down and wrote in the sand, he was playing for time in order to see how the expected response of the crowd or those overhearing could be countered. Perhaps he hoped he would hear a different response instead of the predictable one.

After taking his time and listening to both parties, Jesus decided to take a stand. So how could he challenge the disciples' cultural limitations and the historical prejudice of centuries? The Jews at this time indeed believed that Gentiles were no better than dogs. This is why Jesus used the word 'dog' to address this woman – he wanted to use the same terms that a typical Jew would employ.

To understand this story, and why Jesus took such a stand, we need to look at a saying from the Levant that has existed since antiquity: 'the mother-in-law speaks to the neighbour so that her daughter-in-law may hear'.

As we know, historically and in perhaps all cultures, the relationship between mother-in-law and daughter-in-law can be tense, edgy and sometimes explosive. For the mother-in-law to convey a message to her daughter-in-law without risking either an argument or an abrupt end to any conversation, the only way to do this is to speak loudly to the neighbour so that the daughter-in-law may hear indirectly. In this way, she would not automatically put up barriers, because the message was directed at another. Jesus used the mother-in-law's strategy and spoke to the Syro-Phoenician woman, 'the neighbour', so that the disciples might hear.

He appeared to be affirming the disciples' attitude when he said to the woman, 'It is not fair to take the children's food and throw it to the dogs.' This harsh statement must have had an incredible impact on both sides. For the woman, his words must have been like a slap in the face, while the disciples must have been ecstatic – they were right to have tried to turn her away! I can see Peter, for example, pumping his fist and thinking, 'Yes!

This is our Master and teacher who knows where this woman belongs.'

Jesus' shocking words would have been understandable from the point of view of the disciples, yet it was so much against the nature of Jesus: not how he deals with people who come to him for help!

After throwing this bombshell of a statement, Jesus again took time to see what the reactions would be. The woman would not be defeated; she would empty herself totally in front of Jesus, agreeing with him that she was a dog. She said, 'Yes, Lord, yet even the dogs eat the crumbs that fall from their masters' table.' This amazing and shocking statement was also a bombshell. It is worth noting that Jesus describing her as a dog was greatly offensive and insulting. In the Levant, from that time until even today, dogs existed only on farms or as packs in the wild. People just did not keep them as 'pets'. So at that time, and in that context, Jesus was not talking about a fluffy, clean, cute puppy dog. He was talking about a dirty, dangerous, disease-ridden animal. Now we see the depth of Jesus' statement and her response. He meant to offend, and to provoke the woman, and she meant to fire the very last shot she had. She did not just accept the name of dog, she went even further – to dream like a dog! What would the dog's ultimate dream be, but to devour the scraps and crumbs that may fall from the master's rich table? I imagine that Jesus was now the one to pump his fist and say to himself, 'Yes! I hope this message got through to the 'daughter-in-law' (the disciples)!'

Jesus must have been full of admiration and love for this brave mother. Then he reacted to her in a way that the disciples would never have imagined, commending her for her faith. He answered her, 'Woman, great is your faith! Let it be done for you as you wish.' This would have taught the disciples one of the hardest lessons of their lives. Jesus looked at her faith and her heart rather than at her place of birth or her cultural or religious category. He sweeps away the little boxes of 'in' and 'out', treating her as a human being of equal value to his disciples and his own people. Through this extraordinary encounter, Jesus taught his disciples a hard lesson about who he was – not just the Messiah coming to save the Jews but a Saviour for everybody – as well as to whom his mission was directed. The disciples would remember this incident as long as they lived because Jesus' approach had been so unusual and so apparently out of character.

This story forms a dramatic narrative of an encounter that goes beyond the boundaries of Galilee, where Jesus lived and had his ministry, and demonstrates how Jesus broke boundaries when necessary to demonstrate the culture of God in the cultures of the world. The cultural background of exclusion and intolerance is no different from that found in many parts of the world in the twenty-first century.

Once again we see the culture of God, with his arms outstretched wide to embrace all nations, tribes and tongues. There are no 'outsiders'! We must fundamentally revise our understanding of God to reflect this true nature of the culture of God. Again and again, the message comes loud and clear – there is no 'in' or 'out', no marginalised in God's eyes.

Sadly this story is as relevant to Christians and the Church in the twenty-first century as it was at the time of Christ and in the early Church. We still have all kinds of barriers between insiders and outsiders, between the 'children' and the 'dogs'. The culture of God sees no boundaries, no demarcation, no outcasts and no privileged few. Because of this, Christians, and the Church, should be seen as counter-cultural in every generation, asking the awkward questions – even to the point of being subversive.

We need to be centred in our faith and confident in our identity so that we can react positively when we are challenged by difference in any form. We must reach out and be in the world, with all our love and passion, to serve it and transform it, living fully in God's culture of love rather than human cultures of difference and division.

Mary and Martha

Now as they went on their way, he entered a certain village, where a woman named Martha welcomed him into her home. She had a sister named Mary, who sat at the Lord's feet and listened to what he was saying. But Martha was distracted by her many tasks; so she came to him and asked, 'Lord, do you not care that my sister has left me to do all the work by myself? Tell her then to help me.' But the Lord answered her, 'Martha, Martha, you are worried and distracted by many things; there is need of only one thing. Mary has chosen the better part, which will not be taken away from her.' (Luke 10:38–42)

The story of Mary and Martha is probably one of the most popular stories in the Church because it gives an easy lesson to learn, which is 'listening to Jesus is more important than making him lunch'. But this story actually poses a challenge that could be directed to Jesus himself. Jesus criticised Simon the Pharisee for not showing him any kind of hospitality, while a sinful woman poured her heart out at his feet. In this story, Jesus is almost criticising Martha for working hard to express her hospitality. Make up your mind, Jesus! Are you for or against the showing of hospitality? As usual we have to go beyond what meets the eye to understand how Jesus reacted to the two women, and how he engaged with them on two different levels.

We need to highlight here a couple of observations: the first is that Jesus did not criticise Martha for showing hospitality as such. In fact, Jesus always welcomed acts of hospitality; we see that clearly when he turned water into wine at the wedding in Cana and also when he told Zacchaeus that he wanted to have dinner with him. Jesus was not aloof and withdrawn, and he always accepted people's hospitality – even if they were judged by society as sinners. The second observation is that Martha complained to Jesus about Mary's laziness because she was sitting and listening to him rather than helping with preparations. Only at that point, when she had complained, did Jesus engage lovingly with her, showing her how God thinks in such a situation. In his social engagements and encounters, Jesus did not only deal with the 'here and now'; he always helped his people and, consequently, helps us today to glimpse the mind of God and the culture of God regarding each specific situation. He could have told Martha to leave lunch for later and come and talk now. In this way, he would have dealt with the situation but left us nothing. Who would have written that encounter down?

I lived in Beirut during my theological education and, whenever I went home to Syria, my mother would disappear into the kitchen for hours to prepare every single meal that she knew I liked in order to express her love. I would always say to her, 'Mum, I am here for a short time. I want to see you and be with you. Stop disappearing for hours and hours in the kitchen.' But my mother, coming from the same Middle Eastern culture and background as Mary and Martha, could not help herself. Hospitality was her main way to express her love to those who were dear to her. The food was wonderful, but I would happily have sacrificed the food for some extra time to sit with her.

The culture of God in this story is to be found in Jesus' words when he goes beyond the immediate: 'Martha, Martha, you are worried and distracted by many things; there is need of only one thing. Mary has chosen the better part, which will not be taken away from her.' There was no rebuke, only loving guidance to see a better option in life. In this gentle remark, Jesus acknowledges Martha's need to arrange proper hospitality for her guest, which is the immediate concern, but he took her beyond the immediate, opening up to her what is better and everlasting, a source of strength forever, which is his gift of life which no one can take away. This is the 'one thing' that Jesus was referring to. The culture of God is the culture of Life. Jesus helped Martha to take the better choice, which was life and spirit rather than food and drink. As Jesus said to his disciples, when his disciples were complaining about his teaching, 'It is the spirit that gives life; the flesh is useless. The words that I have spoken to you are spirit and life' (John 6:63). Jesus gives us a direct answer to why he would be the only one able to show us the culture of God: he was with God and he is God before he came to us. He continues to contrast the importance of focusing on the spiritual – our relationship with God – with our own emphasis on matters of the flesh. Only through a spiritual focus can we be part of this divine culture. In the story, it is the contrast between the earthly culture and the divine culture, between the spirit and the flesh. Mary had chosen the spirit, while Martha was weighed down with the concerns of the flesh. Jesus reminded her that the spirit was even better!

This encounter points out that the heart of God desires that we are in communion, in fellowship, in a lively relationship with him. The culture of God calls us to be where the eternal is, where we find lasting truth, as opposed to our transient, earthly cultures. Our final destination is within that divine culture. Remember what Jesus said in the Sermon on the Mount: 'For where your treasure is, there your heart will be also' (Matthew 6:21). In his conversation with Martha, Jesus is challenging the Levantine culture, which could go to an extreme in its emphasis on hospitality. As always, he challenged those extremes just as he challenged the Levantine over-emphasis on the family that we saw before. When he said, 'For I have come to set a man against his father, and a daughter against her mother, and a daughter-in-law against her mother-in-law' (Matthew 10:35), he was not against the family, but he was making a bold and shocking statement to help the people find a balance. As his earthly culture exaggerated, so did Jesus. He was saying to the Levantine culture that you can put nothing before God, not even your family. Your treasure, your heart, should be with God.

In this journey of exploring how Jesus Christ dealt with, reacted to, challenged and guided so many very different and diverse people, we have seen him unpacking the many layers that lie within the culture of God. He shed light on so many different aspects of the divine culture through deep engagement with his own earthly culture, teaching generation after generation as he forged an intimate bond between the divine culture and the earthly cultures in which he lived such a dynamic and passionate life. He brought these two cultures together in dialogue, in contrast, in agreement and even in collision. The result is that we have been given an enormous wealth of teachings and experiences that guide us on our own personal journeys with God.

divine vs. earthly

8

The Crucifixion and the Resurrection

I grew up in a family of six children and our mother was a seamstress. She specialised in making clothes for women who could not wear regular 'off the peg' clothes for various reasons. These women were desperate to wear beautiful dresses just like everyone else, and my mother was able to take a piece of fabric and make a beautiful dress for them. I still recall the joy on the faces of these ladies when they would see themselves in the mirror in these wonderful outfits. I vividly remember how my mother would spread the fabric out, draw lines on it using a piece of soap and a ruler, and then take the scissors and destroy the fabric by cutting it into many pieces. It was a miracle to me how she would take these pieces of fabric and make a beautiful dress, fitting each piece into a three-dimensional item of beauty.

I asked her on many occasions, 'Mum, aren't you afraid that after you cut the fabric you will find out that your lines were wrong?' My mother laughed and told me that she was not worried because she knew what she was doing and that she couldn't make the dress if she didn't cut the fabric up in the first place. In my eyes, she had destroyed the fabric – how on earth could a dress come out of bits of cloth? For my mother, the image of the dress was already in her head, and as she cut the fabric she was realising the potential that lay within it.

Many years later, after I had studied theology and gone deeper into my faith in Christ, I realised my mother's wisdom and skills, and she inspired me through her life and career to understand the Cross and the Resurrection of Jesus Christ in a different way.

I saw humanity as the woman who cannot go to the shop and buy a beautiful dress because nothing fits her. I saw God as the seamstress, and Jesus as the fabric. I realised that there would have been no way to reconcile humanity and God without the destruction of Jesus on the Cross. This is just like my mother – in my eyes – destroying the fabric. Those standing at the Cross saw Jesus destroyed; for them, God 'put the wrong lines on the fabric' and they deserted him. They did not realise that the fabric must be 'destroyed' in order for the dress to emerge. The destruction of that man, Jesus of Nazareth, on the Cross was the way for God to reassemble the pieces into a glorious Resurrection. Even the beloved disciple and Jesus' own mother, who stuck by him through all that had happened, could not see the image that lay within God's mind and the glory that was to come. Only in the culture of God could the full image of the glorious 'dress' take shape.

God showed us in the Resurrection what was eternally in him. He showed humanity that his culture is the culture of eternal life. Throughout the life of Jesus in his earthly culture, God was drawing the lines on the fabric. But the people around Jesus, including the disciples, were like me, looking at those lines but never understanding how they would lead to the beauty that would one day emerge from such great destruction and darkness.

Why such destruction and darkness? Jesus had to face the Cross because of our broken humanity and our sinful nature. What is sin? Sin is our disobedience to God and everything that separates us from God. It is inevitable in the journey that God made from heaven to earth to become one of us that he would face our broken humanity. Humanity resisted his holiness and righteousness. God's very decision to become one of us meant that inevitably, in some form or another, he would face our brokenness. I am not suggesting in any way that death on the

Cross was planned and arranged by God. Jesus did not collaborate with others so that he could be crucified. When he faced the Cross, he was obedient but he was not looking for a spectacular death! Because of his love, he clashed with the evil and corruption of his society – and religion was an essential element of that corruption. As long as Jesus threatened their worldly power, the religious leaders had to kill him; only in this way was the Cross inevitable.

The drawing of the pattern on the fabric, the cutting and the making of the dress, are one process; they are parts of a sequence that cannot be changed. We cannot sew the fabric before we cut it, and if we stop before the final stage then there is no dress, and the pieces have no meaning and no purpose. We should see the life of Jesus, the Cross and the Resurrection as an inseparable whole.

Only through taking the journey of Jesus, from his birth to the Resurrection, can we gain real access to the culture of God. If we stop at the Cross, for example, we have just a story of defeat and devastation; similarly, if we take the life of Jesus without the Cross and the Resurrection then we would be reading merely the life of another teacher in history. In these cases, we would miss much of the culture of God: we see the culture of God in the life and teachings of Jesus because we look at it through the lens of the Resurrection.

As we look at the major steps in the crucifixion of Christ, we can see in a striking way those moments that transcend human thinking and behaviour as God drew out his lines on the fabric of Jesus.

Jesus enters Jerusalem

The first incident that we should examine is when Jesus entered Jerusalem. We see in the Gospel narratives that he was expected to enter the great city as a political leader, bringing a powerful message to challenge the Roman occupation:

'So they took branches of palm trees and went out to meet him, shouting, "Hosanna! Blessed is the one who comes in the name of the Lord – the King of Israel!"' (John 12:13)

Now Jesus stood before the governor; and the governor asked him, 'Are you the King of the Jews?' Jesus said, 'You say so.' (Matthew 27:11)

Jesus' arrival was expected to be nothing less than a signal that the time for liberation was at hand. But Jesus, he who had experienced the culture of God first-hand, went against the current and made a radical statement that was completely at odds with the people's expectations. Instead of arriving on a proud stallion, a symbol of earthly power, he chose to ride a donkey, which in his earthly culture was the symbol of humility and even stupidity; in the Middle East, we call stupid people donkeys too! What a shock this must have been for those who were waiting to welcome their new 'political and military leader'. Jesus was armed with a completely different vision, which came directly from the culture of God.

We take this radical choice of mount for granted today, and we do not see how significant it was, and just how Jesus was demonstrating that God's own thought-processes could be shockingly different from our own. Jesus' arrival in Jerusalem and his demonstration of the culture of God started a series of actions and events that took the whole region by storm and led ultimately to the crucifixion of Jesus.

From that event on, we see a huge scandal unfolding which showed up so clearly the chasm between the culture of God and how the religious leaders had taught people to understand God. This gap was incredibly deep. For example, according to Luke's Gospel narrative, we see that, after he entered Jerusalem, Jesus went to the temple and there he clearly expressed his total rejection of how the religious leaders used the temple as a marketplace. This deepened the rift between Jesus and the religious leaders.

As we look at this event, we see Jesus moving further and further away from 'religion' and clashing with the temple as a profit-making institution: 'He said to them, "It is written, 'My house shall be called a house of prayer'; but you are making it a den of robbers"' (Matthew 21:13).

Jesus revealed at this moment an important element of the culture of God: that the house of the Lord should only be a house of prayer. The culture of God is a culture that values communication: prayer is a relational activity; a way of relating to God; an open, dynamic and lively bond between the Creator and the creation.

This incident shows us that Jesus has completely abandoned the idea of 'religion'. In all his life, he never mentioned the word 'religion'. He clashed with the religious leaders but he did not claim to bring a 'new religion' or that he was reforming the religion that was already there. His emphasis was always on faith and relationship with God. Turning the tables at the temple tells us that he did not come to found a new religion. Religion is organised, and that organisation focuses on power and economy rather than faith. Jesus made it clear that there was no justification for making the house of God an economic entity. He fought the notions of turning faith into a business, and faith wielding worldly power. God does not want the relationship we have with him to be turned into an institution.

The Last Supper

Jesus chose to institute a radically different expression of faith when he offered the bread and wine to the disciples as the new institution of God's covenant with his people. He made his own body the temple and he offered that to humanity. This is what happened in Jerusalem after the table-turning at the temple, when he shared his Last Supper with his friends.

Twice in my life, I felt how Jesus would have felt at the Last Supper. One time was when I was the youth leader in my church in Lattakia, Syria. After some six years, I decided to go to Germany to continue my education. When the youth group discovered that I was leaving, they were furious and deeply saddened. They even tried to plot with my mother to hide my passport so that I could not go! When the day came to say goodbye, our home was filled with young people who remained there overnight. We spent the evening and the night, eating, drinking tea and remembering the times we had spent together, the good moments and the bad, the jokes and all the special times over the six years. I remember that night even today, decades later, as though it happened yesterday. We laughed and we cried, because that night was a time of one of the deepest fellowships I have ever experienced with a group of people. The intimacy with those dear friends caused me profound agony at the thought of leaving them. My soul was saddened because I did not want to leave them. But I had to go. I felt unity with them, and that Christ was uniting us; this went beyond any human description. It was a moment that I could recognise in the clearest way when Jesus said, 'I give you a new commandment, that you love one another. Just as I have loved you, you also should love one another' (John 13:34).

The second time was very similar, when I graduated from the Near East School of Theology in Beirut, where I was also a youth leader. The day before graduation, my youth group came to the school and we had dinner together, which went on until the next morning. We talked about the years of being together in the name of Christ. We laughed and cried as we remembered so many moments that coloured our lives forever.

In both events, I felt that I could understand in a deep, existential way what Jesus and the disciples experienced at the Last Supper. The disciples knew that Jesus would not be with them much longer. They did not know the details, but they knew that their precious time together was coming to an end. This was their last chance to share memories of the three intense years they had spent with their Master, and soon this would all be but memories.

Jesus knew what they were thinking; he felt the intensity of the moment and understood the enormous loss they would all be feeling later. He could not have left them without leaving with them something extraordinary that could unite them forever. When Jesus used the elements that were available to them, such as bread and wine, he filled those vehicles with heavenly culture, putting himself, his presence and his love, inside the bread and wine.

He brought his original culture, the culture of God, and his earthly culture into an eternal embrace. Jesus told the disciples something that they would only understand later, which would remain with generation after generation of Christians: that the culture of God is the culture of eternal fellowship, a culture where there is no place for sorrow, anger, separation, and the darkness of evil that was waiting at the Cross for him. His presence in the bread and the wine are always the source of comfort, joy and hope, which remind us always that we are one with the risen Lord and that our true belonging is where he belongs – which is in the culture of God.

The Last Supper once again reveals that God just thinks differently, and the more we are absorbed by the culture of God then the more we are lost in this wonder of love and self-giving.

I would like to say to Leonardo da Vinci, 'Sorry, my friend. Your painting does not depict the true image of the Last Supper.' Sadly, so many Christians, even in the Levant, have come to regard that painting as an almost perfect depiction of the event itself. First of all, Jesus would have never, ever have sat in the middle of his disciples, with six on his left and six on his right as if they were on the top table, facing a banquet. The Last Supper was a deeply intimate, emotional and heartfelt gathering of friends. Jesus was the servant of his friends, so he would be in a position at the table that would enable him to serve them. They would have sat around a table, with no one seated at its 'head'. Jesus on many occasions revealed, in the culture of God, that Almighty God the Creator can also be, through Jesus, the servant. Jesus lived his entire life serving others, teaching, healing, helping and redeeming. God is great, and at the same time, in his heart, God can be modest, humble, a servant. This shatters the attitude of the religious leaders in Jesus' time.

My second point would be about the place settings on the table. In Leonardo's painting, each person has their own plate, a nice glass beaker rather than a clay cup – and a bread roll. What we see is how Jesus would have dined in sixteenth-century Italy, and we should remember that this might be wonderful art but it is *not* a photograph of the actual scene. I remember very well when Bishop Michael Marshall, the co-founder of my charity (the Awareness Foundation), came with me to visit Syria in around 2004. On the first evening, we sat around a table with my family for dinner. Dinner is not the main meal in the Middle East unless there is a big occasion. Our dinner would be a light meal, without heavy foods like meat. Humus, olives and different dips such as zata (a mix of thyme, other herbs and olive oil) would be on offer, together with a flat bread called khobez. We gave the bishop a plate, and I gave him the option to eat like us or in a European style. He chose to eat as we ate. I said, 'In this case, you don't have a plate!' This is how we eat: after prayer, we take bread and we break it and share the pieces around the table. We don't have individual bread rolls on side plates. Then we all take pieces of bread and we dip them in whatever we like; the dips are shared. After dinner, all the fragments of bread are collected and put away to be used for the next meal. As I mentioned earlier, bread is considered to be grace (a gift from God) in the Middle East. This gave the bishop a taste of just how the Last Supper would have been conducted.

As we were eating, the bishop said to me, 'Now I understand the Last Supper much more! They were all dipping in the same dishes on the table.'

It reminded the bishop of when the disciples were wondering which of them would betray Jesus. 'It is one of the twelve, one who is dipping bread into the bowl with me', Jesus told them

(Mark 14:20). All of them would have been dipping their bread into the same bowl. Jesus' point was not to identify anyone, but to indicate that the person who would betray him was such an intimate and trusted friend that they would have eaten from the same bowl.

Jesus knew who was to betray him, but he included Judas in the Last Supper, his most intimate farewell gathering. Jesus showed love to this disciple to the very end; he did not expose or shame him. How does this measure to our standards today? This gives us such a shocking insight into the heart of God, whose forgiveness really does know no limits, even to the point of sharing loving fellowship with someone who is working to destroy you!

Because of the implications of looking into the heart and the culture of God, we should never think that we have *fully* understood any moment of the life and teachings of Jesus. There is always more to learn. God's heart is limitless, and we can only prayerfully approach and hope to receive a blessing from our efforts to seek deeper meanings in what we read and try to emulate.

Now let's look at the words that Jesus used at the table: 'This is my body' and 'This is my blood'. For any culture, such words would be confusing, upsetting and very hard to accept, because Jesus did not say that these were 'like' his body and blood. These were not to be mere symbols, but a genuine fusing of Jesus and those elements. The idea was a source of fear even for the disciples. In the Gospel according to John, Jesus taught about this in the synagogue in Capernaum, well before the Last Supper: 'Very truly, I tell you, unless you eat the flesh of the Son of Man and drink his blood, you have no life in you. Those who eat my flesh and drink my blood have eternal life, and I will raise them up on the last day; for my flesh is true food and my blood is true drink. Those who eat my flesh and drink my blood abide in me, and I in them' (John 6:53–56). The beloved disciple tells us that after Jesus said this, 'many of his disciples turned back and no longer went about with him' (John 6:66).

Why would Jesus have picked the symbols of bread and wine to represent forever the sacrifice that he was going to face, and why would he associate them with his broken body and the blood he would shed on the Cross? Jesus picked bread and wine because of the ritual around the table, the intimacy of sharing them between family and friends. He went to the most basic staple of human life and community, which is breaking bread and sharing wine. Bread and wine are the most basic products of human labour, a symbol of working together as a community. They symbolise relationships between people, which are at the root of all earthly cultures; relationships are also at the heart of the Trinity and the culture that flowed from it. Breaking bread and sharing wine is a celebration of community life and it shows interaction, intimacy, fellowship and caring – all of which are also part of the Trinity and the culture of God.

The analogy becomes perfect. You would only see the whole loaf of flat bread before the meal and the fellowship began, and the meal would begin with the breaking of the bread. The reconciliation with God would not occur without the breaking of the body of Jesus. The dress could not be made without the cutting of the fabric. The same could be said of the wine. Unless the grapes are crushed, the juice fermented and the wineskin or jar opened, no one can drink. Jesus picked those symbols because they were understood and used on a daily basis by his earthly culture. He knew that those who heard would not fully understand the symbolism behind his words until after the Cross and the Resurrection.

We can see that those images go far beyond the human understanding of fellowship and community. They tell us how God himself exists. 'Those who eat my flesh and drink my blood abide in me, and I in them' (John 6:56). In the final prayer of his long discourse, in John 17:21, Jesus says 'As you, Father, are in me and I am in you, may they also be in us, so that the world may believe that you have sent me.' We see here that Jesus is talking about the oneness of the people of faith in him and the Father. Abiding in Jesus means being rooted in him in a way that, although we live in the world and in our cultures, we also need to belong to the culture of God. Since we do not have Jesus any longer in the flesh, in the power of the Spirit we are united in the body and blood, which is the very meeting point between the cultures of the world and the culture of God.

Looking at the Levantine culture of Jesus opens the door for us to explore deeper the culture of God. Thinking back to my two suppers in Syria and Lebanon, I do not think that their vivid memories will ever diminish, even to the end of my life. Therefore, I can understand how the disciples would have thought about the Last Supper as long as they lived, and that its impact upon them would never have lessened. The people of the Levant, filled with emotion and passion, invest a lot of time and energy in their relationships, and the only way to look deeper into the culture of God is to unpack this rich and intense culture. The Levant today still shares a significant amount of culture, customs and turns of phrase with the earthly culture of Jesus.

Symbolism and imagery are essential to the Levantine culture. Whenever we talk, we draw verbal pictures to convey our message. We use analogies a lot. Our language is very visual, decorative and poetic. When I learnt English, I also had to learn to leave such flowery language behind. Jesus could surprise even those who spent their lives talking in this way, and his analogies of bread and wine stirred the disciples and took them into a new level of relationship with God. The culture of God raises even the simplest to new heights, and all the details of our lives become potential vehicles of grace, teaching us more how we can connect to the culture of God.

The Garden of Gethsemane

After the Last Supper, we see Jesus withdrawing from public life and taking his intimate friends to the Garden of Gethsemane for a time of reflection and prayers. The prayers that Jesus said in Gethsemane go beyond what is mere obedience to God. Faithful people like Abraham have given us terrific examples of obedience to God – and also resistance. But here we see a new dimension that comes from Jesus having the culture of God within him, and that is dealing with the will of God. He was in a conversation with God the Father, stating what he would have liked if he had the choice as a human being, and this shows us the deep human vulnerability of Jesus. He showed the Father the weakness of being under the limitations of a physical human body. He did not play the superman who knew everything and who could be affected by nothing. He opened himself totally to the Father, with all the struggle that was taking place in his heart and mind as he was heading towards the final human frontier: death. At the very same time, he was fully aware that what he would like to avoid, simply the depth of suffering, could not be avoided if the Father so willed. What Jesus did was to lay down his humanity in the hands of the Father and then acknowledge that the will of the Father is in every way superior to his will as a human being. He asked the Father so that his will might be fulfilled. This has revealed a totally new dimension in communication with God, which is recognising that what I want may not always be identical to what God wants for me.

> 'My Father, if it is possible, let this cup pass from me; yet not what I want but what you want.' (Matthew 26:39)

> 'My Father, if this cannot pass unless I drink it, your will be done.' (Matthew 26:42)

The strength that Jesus sought in this prayer came from his faith, which was that the will of the Father, even if it contradicted his own will, would always be the best. This kind of openness to the culture of God is beyond how human beings would have ever thought to approach God. Today, through Christ and through learning how Christ himself prayed, and being fully aware of belonging to the culture of God, we have the faith that also through him we belong to that culture and can approach God in the same way. This is beyond obedience: it is a dynamic relationship that values both wills – ours and God's. Like Jesus, we can only seek to know God's will, to invite him to have the central place in our lives and to ask him to guide us. If you want to know the will of God, have a good and dynamic relationship with him and know your own will. The closer we become to God, the closer will our own will be to his.

I experienced this very much during the war in Lebanon; I constantly asked myself, 'What on earth am I doing here, studying in hell?' Yes, I was young and adventurous, but being in the middle of street-fighting in a civil war is not the usual adventure that a young man would want to embark on. I still don't know how I did it. At the time, my desire was to finish my theological education. I did not know what God wanted from me – I was too immature in every way. I was faced with a dilemma: to continue my education in the midst of extreme violence and sectarianism or to drop everything and go back home and hope to find another way to complete my studies. In the end, I stayed and continued my education, finding the strength from God to finish my task. I put my trust in him that his will be done, not mine.

God helps us to make our will and his will come together. Only through him can we do that.

The trial of Jesus

In the middle of the turmoil that surrounded Jesus during his trial, and especially his encounter with the military Prefect who ruled the small province of Judaea, Pontius Pilate, Jesus helps us to see another unique aspect of the culture of God.

He was brought to Pilate to be judged and sentenced to death. But Pilate looked into the case and found no reasons to sentence

Jesus to death. There are three main 'players' in this scene. The first major 'player' is the Pharisees, who were working tirelessly to whip the crowd into a fury against Jesus. They were weaving a trap around him, telling blatant lies to push Pilate to condemn him – 'We found this man perverting our nation, forbidding us to pay taxes to the emperor, and saying that he himself is the Messiah, a king' (Luke 23:2) – and even using the politics and principles of the Roman Empire itself to threaten the Roman leader – 'the Jews cried out, "If you release this man, you are no friend of the emperor. Everyone who claims to be a king sets himself against the emperor"' (John 19:12).

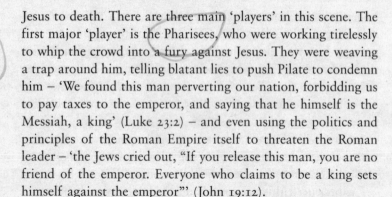

The second 'player' was Pilate, who found himself in the middle of this weird situation. On one hand, he repeatedly found no grounds to the religious leaders' accusations, while on the other he was considering the consequences for himself if the troubles escalated out of control should he fail to act. 'Then Pilate said to the chief priests and the crowds, "I find no basis for an accusation against this man." But they were insistent and said, "He stirs up the people by teaching throughout all Judea, from Galilee where he began even to this place"' (Luke 23:4–5). Pilate was extremely hesitant to listen to the religious leaders because somehow he felt it was not right or within the law to kill Jesus. Do not think of Pilate as the 'good guy' who understood Jesus and took his side. He was trying to do his job and represent the Empire while keeping the peace.

The third 'player' is Jesus, who used two methods of dealing with the storm that was roaring around him. He had used both methods before. His first method was silence, when he listened to everyone around him. The second was to use very brief sentences and statements, sometimes reflecting the questions back onto the questioner – 'Then Pilate asked him, "Are you the king of the Jews?" He answered, "You say so"' (Luke 23:3) – and at other times challenging those around him –'Jesus answered him, "You would have no power over me unless it had been given you from above; therefore the one who handed me over to you is guilty of a greater sin'" (John 19:11). Through both methods, Jesus brought the religious leaders and the political leader into comparison with each other, and the result is surprising – here we see the religious leaders, who were supposedly living by God's principles of honesty, truth and mercy, in reality conspiring and lying, abusing their responsibilities to stir up the people in order to bring about the death of an innocent man, and the Roman military leader, supposedly a brutal, selfish and unclean pagan, trying to be fair and to uphold the law, and being honest with the religious leaders, with himself and with Jesus. Jesus is presenting us with a deep and incredible comparison between the ugly face of corrupt religion and the fair face of secular society.

Although Jesus was fully aware that he was heading towards the Cross, he shows both in his silence and in his statements a great and powerful inner peace and confidence. This takes us back to the time when he was with the disciples on the boat in the midst of the storm and was sleeping. Of course, he was aware of the storm; but he was demonstrating inner peace while his disciples panicked. On that occasion, he rebuked the wind and the waves and he calmed the storm. Now, at a trial with his own life at stake, he demonstrated his inner peace again. This is the very same peace that he gave to us when he said, 'Peace I leave with you; my peace I give to you. I do not give to you as the world gives. Do not let your hearts be troubled, and do not let them be afraid' (John 14:27).

The quality of this peace is beyond any human ability to create; it belongs to the heart of the culture of God. In today's world we find ourselves constantly in storms and turmoil, and we look for peace. But there is no source for this special peace without being connected to the culture of God. The kind of peace that Jesus showed during his trial is ours only through him. How do we receive this peace? We do so when we become citizens of the culture of God and we receive the power of the Holy Spirit. The source of this peace is nothing less than God the Holy Spirit, who is active in us and in the Church, the body of believers, the Body of Christ.

The Cross

The court continued, the trap was sprung, and Jesus would indeed face his destruction on the Cross. The lines continued to be drawn on the fabric, and at the Cross the scissors would begin their work. As the fabric is at last cut apart, as Jesus faces the last moments of his human life, enduring the ultimate fear of any human being, the fear of death, he illuminates our existence with a fresh pearl of the culture of God. In another statement directed to his Father, Jesus prays not for himself but for those who are killing him. Jesus lived what he taught. He had taught his disciples and those around him to 'Love your enemies, and pray for those who persecute you' (Matthew 5:44) and here he was, lifting those words to the heart of the Father, 'Father, forgive them; for they do not know what they are doing' (Luke 23:34).

Love and forgiveness are integral not only to God's commandments, but to the inner life of the Trinity. It can be so hard for us to forgive someone who has done us a significant wrong. It is definitely stretching our humanity to ask us to forgive those who are persecuting us. No other philosophy, religion or school of thought asks this. God came to us to show us the way, how to become one with the culture of God and live accordingly.

At my theology school in Beirut, we lost three friends to the war: a theology student, a member of our youth group, and a fellow university student. When we gathered to talk about each one I remember very, very well the physical pain of forgiving those who'd killed our friends. It is such a great accomplishment even to say to myself, 'I forgive them.' I could not have fully appreciated what Jesus said on the Cross unless I had experienced great wrongs myself. I wanted to forgive, and I focused on Jesus' words, but there was an incredible force of anger within me and the turmoil was unbearable. I saw the senseless loss caused by idiotic violence, and inside I had a hurricane of anger against this dirty war around me. I had to centre myself in Jesus and say, 'I want to forgive.' The struggle is unbelievable. I remember sitting in my room at the school of theology and crying and crying and crying, trying to find equilibrium inside me, some kind of peace, some kind of balance. I remember that I cried in the depths of many nights, trying to make sense of what God wanted from me, and struggling between abandoning everything and holding on to find the purpose, the road that God was leading me on and accepting that I had to walk that road. Was I sure I was on the road? No. I screamed at God, 'I will stake my life on that inner conviction that you have a purpose for me and are leading me somewhere!' Something in me told me that this was the path God wanted for me, and I took that choice.

God loves humanity, and he walks with humanity to the end. The culture of God is the culture of a love covenant that challenges us to go beyond our barriers and our borders. Having lived directly through at least five different wars in my life, from civil war to conflict between nations, I learnt the hard way what the word 'forgiveness' could mean. Having also lost dear friends in those wars, it was enormously difficult to find that inner peace which could lead to that forgiveness. You cannot forgive if you are angry, if you hate, or if the storm has you in its grasp.

In my youth group in Beirut, which met every Saturday no matter how bad the fighting was, we had three or four street-fighters who used to leave their weapons in the reception area before coming to our meeting. They were Christians and non-Christians. They insisted on coming and being part of this group, because they felt that they could be in touch with themselves on a different level thanks to God's presence with us. The culture of God was present among us, and God helped the streetfighters to find that inner peace; they abandoned their guns and turned their backs on the fighting. I saw this with my own eyes, I lived it, and it was so hard to talk about forgiveness with those fighters. When one of the youth group was killed in an explosion when he rushed to the aid of the wounded, it was tough to talk about why God allowed this to happen, and how we could forgive those who were responsible. My effort was to keep the storm out and concentrate on how to receive the divine power of forgiveness. We studied how Jesus lived what he taught. Someone had done this before, and this was a great empowerment and inspiration for us. Jesus was not a mere 'talker'; he became one of us, and he did these things so that we would have the courage today to forgive. That was something essential I learnt in the war about forgiveness, which came from Jesus' own forgiveness when he kept saying from the Cross, 'Father forgive.' In the original version of the Gospel, which was written in Greek, Jesus kept repeating this over and over again. I learnt that forgiveness does not only liberate the one who offended or hurt you, it liberates you from your own darkness. When we are hurt, the anger inside us becomes like a fog that engulfs us and prevents any light from reaching us. Forgiveness is working on this fog to dispel it and allow the light of God to warm our hearts again. This is a process of loving God, loving ourselves and then loving the other.

The last words that Jesus said before the fabric was ultimately sundered was, 'It is finished.' 'Then he bowed his head and gave up his spirit' (John 19:30). The word that St John used in Greek could also mean 'it is accomplished', 'it is complete' or 'it is fulfilled'. What would that mean, and what does it show us about the culture of God?

The fulfilment of Jesus' mission is the new age of grace and the time when the culture of God is manifested in our own human culture. The Cross ended the age of the Law as the mediator between God and humanity and as the way to fulfil God's commandments. As Jesus had said 'Do not think that I have come to abolish the law or the prophets; I have come not to abolish but to fulfil. For truly I tell you, until heaven and earth pass away, not one letter, not one stroke of a letter, will pass from the law until all is accomplished' (Matthew 5:17–18). Many people quote this verse, mistakenly believing that here Jesus is saying that the Law will last forever and that the Bible is the ultimate authority. If this were the case, then Jesus would have accomplished nothing at all. When Jesus said that 'It is finished', he actually said, according to the Greek language in the Gospel according to John, that 'it is complete' or 'accomplished' forever. That is the precise moment when the Law ceased to have authority over humanity, the moment of salvation is completed and everything that went before it is no longer binding. The ultimate authority for those who believe in the person of Christ is Christ himself. The accomplishment of the Law and the beginning of the age of grace mark the opening of the gates of the culture of God. We should never quote the Law today as if it has power over our lives. It is dangerous to assume that just because the Law is in the Bible that it remains an appropriate way to fulfil God's commandments. The Law is fulfilled, and after the Resurrection of Jesus our authority is not in a book or a set of laws; it is in the risen and living Lord himself. The culture of God could never have been accessed by us if Jesus had never been born among us. The culture of God, which is beyond the realm of any laws or regulations, is free and it liberates us from all that tries to limit our living, dynamic relationship with God.

The Resurrection

Christians are the people of the Resurrection, not the people of the Cross. We should not seek suffering in our lives in order to 'carry our Cross', but if and when life throws hard times at us and we find ourselves facing a storm, we do indeed carry the Cross. We carry it because we know that Jesus rose again and that his Cross was not the last word of the story of God visiting us. Jesus defeated death and rose again. This is the faith of Christians and the Church, generation after generation.

We need to admit that Christians differ in the way they

understand the event of the Resurrection. The meaning of the Resurrection varies from believing that Jesus rose from the dead in the flesh to believing that the Resurrection is an 'idea'.

The Resurrection of Christ is the ultimate manifestation of the culture of God as the culture of eternal life. It is the culture that changed our cultures radically by giving us the possibility of exploring the mind, the heart and the passion of God. Upon the Cross, we scarred God forever. In the Resurrection, God welcomed the scarred risen Lord back to the divine culture.

In the twenty-first century, nearly two thousand years after the crucifixion of Jesus, of course we can afford to look at an event like the Resurrection with plenty of scepticism, and we can also afford to intellectualise, abstract and mythologise it. Now, we can do whatever we want. But before we do that, let's ask ourselves what really happened. The devastated, defeated and demoralised bunch of uneducated people who had followed a man for three years before seeing him go to his awful, agonising death on the Cross had naturally gone back to their families and their work. So what force could suddenly fire them up to the extent that they would turn the Roman Empire on its head? None of them possessed the intellectual ability to plot and weave such an incredible story, that 'Jesus rose from the dead'. And which of them would be ready to die for such a self-created fantasy? We know that most of the disciples died for their faith. During my life in the Middle East, I met many people who were ready to go to their deaths for their political or ideological beliefs. But none of them would have done that while knowing that their beliefs were false.

The Levant is known for those of its people who would sacrifice their lives for their faiths. As the phenomenon of suicide-bombing started to attract great attention from the Western media, I started one of my sermons at my church in London, England, by asking the people the following question: how many of you are ready to die for your faith? At the end of the service, some people said that my question was too severe and that it made them uncomfortable; the congregation believed that no one today needed to face such a challenge. Years later, and after the deaths of so many Christians in the Middle East, many of those who were at that service still remember my question; now, they understand it. Even in the twenty-first century, Christians are still dying because of their beliefs.

Knowing the culture of the Levant, it would have been absolutely impossible in every way for people like the disciples to have shaken an empire and to have willingly sacrificed their lives merely to keep up a pretence or a fantasy that 'Jesus rose, but only in their hearts'. The very idea of the disciples experiencing the Resurrection 'in their hearts' as a metaphorical restoration of Jesus' life is a cultural impossibility. I do not believe that the disciples could have gained such strength from the metaphorical restoration of a defeated man that they would be moved to change the whole world – or to die for it. If they had only experienced a warm feeling, why lie and pretend that Jesus had come back and was frequently meeting them in the flesh? Honesty would have been the only sensible policy.

Why did the disciples sacrifice themselves for their faith in the risen Lord? I believe that this can only be because they did indeed encounter the risen Jesus. A question we could ask today and at the time of the disciples is, what makes Christians ready to lay down their lives? I know that people of other faiths and ideologies do this, but I am specifically asking about Christians. This is the same question I ask myself today when I go to the Levant, knowing that I could face death at any time there. I believe that the answer lies not only in the empty tomb, but in encounters with the risen Lord. Let's look at the disciples' encounters that freed them from their fear and isolation with such enormous power.

These extraordinary encounters show us that the man who was born and who taught and lived with them did indeed belong to the culture of God, and that culture is the culture of life and power that can overcome even death in every way – physically and spiritually. The Resurrection of Jesus completed the final step of making the dress glorious. The Resurrection also tells us that the very same man who revealed the culture of God in our culture is physically and spiritually back with God, back in his original culture. Why is this important? Because the physical Resurrection of Jesus Christ released the magnificent power of hope in believers throughout history. Our hope in eternal life is real, not intellectual, spiritual or metaphorical, and this is the value of the physical Resurrection of Jesus. We will not be ghosts, because the physical world was transformed and redeemed by the power of Jesus' Resurrection. The fact that Jesus rose from the dead, physically, which is so clearly testified to in all four narratives of the Gospel, means that he was not merely a ghost hovering around. When we die and we are raised with him, we will also be like him, receiving a glorious body like his.

It is helpful to look at some of those encounters that the disciples had with the risen Jesus, to shed some light on the importance and the value of the reality of the Resurrection and the presence of Jesus in his glorified body among them, the true ambassador of the culture of God. They wrote these stories and encounters to passionately share with us their excitement in being there with the risen Lord, talking to him, interacting with him, and even eating and drinking with him. This fellowship is the heart of why the disciples were passionate to convey the message to us, and to include us in the wider fellowship of the risen Master. We are not reading passively, and envying the disciples for their magnificent experiences, but rather feeling that we are one with them in this faith of the One who opened up the heart of God, the culture of the Trinity.

After these things Jesus showed himself again to the disciples by the Sea of Tiberias; and he showed himself in this way. Gathered there together were Simon Peter, Thomas called the Twin, Nathanael of Cana in Galilee, the sons of Zebedee, and two others of his disciples. Simon Peter said to them,

'I am going fishing.' They said to him, 'We will go with you.' They went out and got into the boat, but that night they caught nothing.

Just after daybreak, Jesus stood on the beach; but the disciples did not know that it was Jesus. Jesus said to them, 'Children, you have no fish, have you?' They answered him, 'No.' He said to them, 'Cast the net to the right side of the boat, and you will find some.' So they cast it, and now they were not able to haul it in because there were so many fish. That disciple whom Jesus loved said to Peter, 'It is the Lord!' When Simon Peter heard that it was the Lord, he put on some clothes, for he was naked, and jumped into the lake. But the other disciples came in the boat, dragging the net full of fish, for they were not far from the land, only about a hundred yards off. (John 21:1–8)

Let's look at what made the disciples go back to work after the Cross. Undoubtedly, they felt depressed, defeated and shocked. The loss of their teacher and friend would have been devastating. In order to distract themselves from their great pain and sadness, Peter suggested that they go fishing. At least they could keep busy, wrestling with the sea, and of course with a lot of memories from when Jesus was with them at and around the sea.

History repeats itself, and here is another night recorded in the Gospel where the disciples caught nothing and by the break of dawn were tired and probably fed up. On another occasion, when Jesus called Peter to be his disciple, having asked Peter to sail to the deep and cast the net, Peter being Peter, impulsive and passionate, had said: 'Master, we have worked all night long but have caught nothing. Yet if you say so, I will let down the nets' (Luke 5:5).

Now, Jesus appears again at the seashore, asking them if they had caught anything and telling them to lower their nets again. John (the disciple whom Jesus loved) realised the meaning of the great catch that followed because he had witnessed the earlier time when Jesus asked Peter to cast the net before telling him that, 'from now on you will be catching people' (Luke 5:10). John turned to Peter and said with great awe and excitement 'It is the Lord!' Rather than bringing the boat back, Peter jumped into the lake and just swam for the shore.

It is interesting to look at this again, but from the risen Lord's perspective. Jesus, alone at the shore, looked at his tired, confused and despairing disciples, and he saw that they had caught nothing. Jesus would have felt pity for them; with deep affection and love, he wanted to remind them of a similar encounter from before. So he asked them about their catch. Of course, he knew the answer, and he heard what he had expected. They had caught nothing. So he continued his gentle teasing of the disciples' spirit, asking them to cast their net on the other side of the boat. He was waiting to see when they would recognise who he was, and who would be the first to know him. We need to understand that you would only do this with people you love; Jesus wanted them to learn who he was, and to see the sparkle of surprise and joy when they realised.

> When they had gone ashore, they saw a charcoal fire there, with fish on it, and bread. Jesus said to them, 'Bring some of the fish that you have just caught.' So Simon Peter went aboard and hauled the net ashore, full of large fish, a hundred and fifty-three of them; and though there were so many, the net was not torn. Jesus said to them, 'Come and have breakfast.' Now none of the disciples dared to ask him, 'Who are you?' because they knew it was the Lord. Jesus came and took the bread and gave it to them, and did the same with the fish. This was now the third time that Jesus appeared to the disciples after he was raised from the dead. (John 21:9–14)

Jesus gave them food, reminding them that they still needed sustenance for the journey ahead. He chose bread and fish also to remind them of previous incidents when he fed the five thousand and the four thousand using the same foodstuffs. This is, for me, a lesson that the food that Jesus gives is not only enough for nine thousand people, but that this symbolic gesture of Jesus points at him giving us forevermore the gift of the culture of God, flowing from his life, his teachings, and who he is. The bread and the fish, which were multiplied by the grace of God, are a symbol for the presence of the culture of God in our cultures, which can multiply to sustain every one of us on our journey.

This part of the story, although it does not convey many lessons or teachings, is significant because it emphasises to us today the quality and the nature of such encounters with the risen Lord as true and real meetings with one who is now back in his original culture. The Resurrection, in every incident, testifies to the culture of God, which is the dominion of the Trinity. Jesus is revealing to them that, in the culture of God, there is no death and that his culture is only a culture of life and light. His victory is over the power of darkness and ultimately the power of death. This encounter is like a stone thrown into the pond of history and today we are still living with the ripples; believers continue to experience the presence of the risen Jesus today.

The Road to Emmaus

This elaborate story of the Resurrection that Luke tells reminds me of the elaborate story he tells about the birth of Jesus. He talks about the shepherds and the angels, and he writes an exciting story to present to us the birth of a king, the birth of God on earth. At the end of his narrative, Luke surprises us again with a magnificent account of the two disciples on the road to Emmaus. Here, we need to look back on the power of the *story* and the *storyteller*. We have previously looked at the meaning of these in the Levant. Although Luke was a physician, he was also an artist according to the Christian tradition. In this story, we see a profound example of storytelling which combines the details of the journey of the two disciples on the road from being perplexed, confused and trying to discern what is happening, to the climax of Jesus revealing himself through the breaking of bread and then appearing to them when they met the other disciples. Luke combines this educated way of writing an exciting story with a magnetic plot. This gives this chapter such an impact, making Luke's point by celebrating the risen Master, the risen Jesus.

Every time I try to tell my own story of my journey out of the Levant, I find myself telling it exactly like Luke. My journey was to me so similar to the disciples' journey to Emmaus, a passage from doubt, fear and confusion with a young, fragile faith to maturity and awareness. The Lord was with me on my journey and, at the beginning, I could not recognise him – especially in the middle of warfare and violence – but I could feel the presence of his power and the influence of his guiding hand despite my uncertainty. He was there, he was guiding me, but only now can I look back and understand the impact of that journey on my life. I totally understand the disciples' confusion; even though I was leading a youth group, I was still very young and inexperienced, and we were all trying to discern the Lord's presence together.

What kept the disciples from recognising Jesus? They were so imprisoned in their disappointment that the one they had thought would liberate them physically and politically had been brutally defeated and killed. He died without a fight, and without rousing the people to resistance. Their sorrow and hopelessness became a barrier between them and the Lord, a blindfold that stopped them recognising their travelling companion. They were preoccupied with their own situation, and they could never have expected to see Jesus walking with them. When Jesus asked them, 'What are you discussing with each other while you walk along?' (Luke 24:17), their answer – 'Are you the only stranger in Jerusalem who does not know the things that have taken place there in these days?' (Luke 24:18) – shows that the death of Jesus must have been the talk of the city and that he had had more followers than we usually assume.

When our uncertainty and fear become walls around us, we lose our connection with God, we shut all the doors and bar the windows, not looking beyond the walls that surround us; the culture of God is shut out and we are imprisoned in our own fears. At this time, we need God to break in and find us at our point of need. I do remember when I was at my lowest during the Lebanese Civil War that I entered into this state of loneliness, as though I existed in a soundproof room, and I felt that I had no connection with God and could not reach him. I was lost in my own sorrow. At such times, we see nothing but sorrow and we are for a while blinded to everything else. No messages reach us.

One helping hand for me was my theological education, which was unfolding the Word of God. Working with young people, I was pushed to convey to them what I had been struggling with, but in a positive and encouraging light. At that time, God found me also in that situation through those young people who reflected back to me what I see now as the culture of God, the culture of hope, of enthusiasm for life. I can see the incredible power that broke down all the barriers that surrounded the disciples on the road to Emmaus when Jesus broke bread with them. Traditionally, we understand this as an act of the Eucharist, Communion or the Lord's Supper that we celebrate regularly in church. But I want to make it wider than seeing Jesus as the eucharistic Minister. I see Jesus' breaking the bread as nothing less than his breaking everything that kept them from recognising him. It is a fusion of the earthly culture and the divine culture in that piece of bread, breaking the earthly sorrows and breaking in the culture of God, which helps us to recognise the real presence of the risen Lord in our lives so that each one's whole life becomes the Eucharist. Jesus is constantly celebrating both the breaking of our disappointment and sorrow and the breaking in of God himself and his culture of love and reconciliation into our earthly lives and cultures.

The breaking of the bread with the two disciples is an eternal dialogue between the Cross and the Resurrection in our lives, a constant encounter between the continuous 'crosses' that life throws at us, and the risen Lord who always empowers us with the culture of God to overcome those 'crosses'.

9

A New Culture of Life

Three times in my life, I have experienced first-hand the effects of war and violence on young people: in Lebanon, Syria and Iraq. I saw in the eyes of young people a broken spirit and a destroyed soul that paralysed them; they did not know how to move beyond the disasters around them and they could see no hope in the days and years ahead. They were powerless, frozen in the shadow of the terror and horror that they had experienced. I have seen highly skilled young men and women with no remaining ability to reason or to encompass even the slightest possibility of changing their reality. They saw themselves as helpless and hopeless, surrounded by darkness. They were terrified to take any step. I could identify with their situation because when I had lived in Lebanon the only way that I could break free from this powerless state was through my faith: it was not my own power that could save me, but the power of God, the promise that the Holy Spirit was in us. I had to access this promise; otherwise, my faith would have been totally meaningless. Unless I could believe in the risen Lord and in that darkness take a real 'leap of faith', my faith was useless.

Many years later, in 2016, one of the young men in Syria asked me what right I had to stand before him and the young people gathered there and teach them to be Ambassadors for Peace in a war zone while I could go back to my comfortable life in London, leaving them to face the enormous tragedy of the Syrian Civil War. I told him that he was right to ask this. It is so easy for someone to come from a safe existence in the West, teach about hope and faith, and then get on the first plane back to safety with a big sigh of relief. What gave me the right to teach them was that I had faced seven years of city fighting and war in my own youth, and that I had experienced the same existential challenges of violence and the likelihood of death that they were now facing. All I could do was witness to them and share with them my own, similar experiences so that they might be encouraged. Considering what I went through in my youth, the only power that made me take steps towards the light of hope was the Holy Spirit that moved within me. Being empowered by the Holy Spirit doesn't make the problems disappear, a magic that makes everything flowery and 'nice'. It is the power that makes you identify the chains of hopelessness and fear, and see them as obstacles that you can overcome. The Holy Spirit empowered me when I opened myself to its work, and it enabled me to desire to get beyond my terrible situation. The Holy Spirit is always ready to amaze us with the realisation that we are not alone. As we work to overcome our chains, we start to feel lighter as the chains break away.

When I was studying in Beirut in the 1980s, my classroom learning was not an academic exercise to get a degree in theology – it was a transformative process that moved me from hopelessness to hope. It gave me the tools that we all need; the help that can empower us to access the power within us. In the same way, the apostles needed the physical empowerment of the Holy Spirit in the incident of Pentecost. Pentecost, or the Feast of Fifty Days, is a Jewish festival that marks fifty days after Passover. Only when the disciples were filled with power could they bear witness to the cosmic events of the Cross and the Resurrection and the redemption of creation in Jesus Christ.

When the day of Pentecost came, they were all together in one place. Suddenly a sound like the blowing of a violent wind came from heaven and filled the whole house where they were sitting. They saw what seemed to be tongues of fire that separated and came to rest on each of them. All of them were filled with the Holy Spirit and began to speak in other tongues as the Spirit enabled them.

Now there were staying in Jerusalem God-fearing Jews from every nation under heaven. When they heard this sound, a crowd came together in bewilderment, because each one heard their own language being spoken. Utterly amazed, they asked: 'Aren't all these who are speaking Galileans? Then how is it that each of us hears them in our native language? Parthians, Medes and Elamites; residents of Mesopotamia, Judea and Cappadocia, Pontus and Asia, Phrygia and Pamphylia, Egypt and the parts of Libya near Cyrene; visitors from Rome (both Jews and converts to Judaism); Cretans and Arabs – we hear them declaring the wonders of God in our own tongues!' Amazed and perplexed, they asked one another, 'What does this mean?' (Acts 2:1–12, NIV)

Ever since the Ascension, the disciples had been living in fear, in that upper room behind closed doors. But the Holy Spirit broke in to their self-imposed prison and destroyed the barriers of doubt and fear that had come between their faith and the waiting world. What we read in Acts chapter 2 is a powerful witness to a real experience of liberation. The power of Pentecost released the timid disciples from their doubt and fear and from the limitations of their own culture and language, converting them into fearless and articulate missionaries, on fire with the love of the Spirit. Little wonder that they appeared at first sight as if they were drunk.

If we look at this incident, and see how it is recorded, then there is no shadow of doubt that the essence of the whole book of the Acts of the Apostles was the Acts of the Holy Spirit through the apostles! It is the story of God in action, the story of the culture of God being in direct contact with the culture of the early Church. It is the ultimate revelation that the culture of God can be accessed and lived and witnessed to only through the power of the Holy Spirit, who is God in action.

What happened next? Peter, the fisherman from the north, suddenly finds his tongue and eloquently delivers the message of Christ. The disciples addressed those who had gathered from near and far, expressing their passion and enthusiasm for their faith. St Peter's quote from Joel is central to the universality of the Gospel of Christ: 'this is what was spoken through the prophet Joel: "In the last days it will be, God declares, that I will pour out my Spirit upon all flesh …"' (vv. 16–17)

What happened to me in Lebanon, and to the young people in the shattered countries of Syria and Iraq, is nothing less than an echo of the original Pentecost and proof that God is still in action and that the culture of God is still with us. The culture of God can be embraced through the power of the Holy Spirit. I saw in some of the young people's eyes the sparkle of transformation when they moved from hopelessness to hope. One young man in Syria wrote on his Facebook page, 'Before the training to be an Ambassador for Peace, I was dead and now I am alive again.'

We must realise that the physical absence of Jesus, their leader and mentor whom they had followed for years, had left the disciples bereft. The loss of this extraordinary, charismatic character, who had filled the disciples with courage and power, who had shown such tenderness and love towards the people of the Levant – especially the marginalised and the poor, who never received mercy from any of their leaders – and who had faced the religious leaders with immense wisdom and strength, had a huge impact on the disciples. We should not underestimate the shock they would have suffered when they lost this young man after just three years, only to have him return to them in the most miraculous way, filling them with joy before departing physically for the last time. Jesus had always explained everything to them; they would ask him questions – many more than we read about in the New Testament – for hours and days, and he would patiently teach them. That was his mission – to prepare them for his physical departure and to leave with them his life and teachings, which would lead them to the culture of God that he had lived and shown and taught throughout his time with them.

Yet even after all this, the disciples lacked the courage to face the world, especially the fury of the religious and political system that had crucified their Lord and Master. Before this point, they had never had to face these challenges themselves, and they needed help. During his life, Jesus promised them that he would leave the Comforter with them, the power of the Holy Spirit. They could never have imagined the colossal responsibility that landed on their shoulders after he left them, nor the power of the Holy Spirit which would fill them. After Pentecost, we see the culture of God in action within them. The culture of God is the culture of *life*, the most profound revelation of the Resurrection. In God, there is no death and life is eternal – not eternal in a temporal way, but through the eternal fellowship and living relationship with God. We often understand eternal life as life as we live it now, but never-ending, living endlessly. The word 'eternal' has nothing to do directly with time. It is a quality of life that is beyond the dimension of time. Our life and existence will be with God and in God outside all the dimensions of space and time. The word 'eternal' means deathless, timeless life. It will not feel like an eternity! The Resurrection of Jesus brought God in a new way to the disciples: God directly broke the barrier of death. They saw Jesus, they ate with him and talked to him; he was not a ghost or a 'spirit' but a reality. Eternal life became real. Jesus showed them a state of being that went far beyond time and space. He appeared to them in different ways to tell them that, through him, they had moved from a limited physical existence to unlimited life.

As we look at the descending of the Holy Spirit in light of the culture of God, we see the absolute fulfilment of what Jesus says (John 5:24): 'Very truly, I tell you, anyone who hears my word and believes him who sent me has eternal life, and does not come under judgement, but has passed from death to life.' In hindsight, we can see why John repeatedly writes about eternal life in his Gospel narration. The disciples had experienced this first-hand, coming face to face with eternal life in what Jesus preached and when he came back from the dead.

The culture of God is not something theoretical. We can experience it through our fellowship with God through Jesus Christ, by the power of the same Holy Spirit that moved the disciples to go out and face the world.

The result of encountering the culture of God as the culture of life must be transformative, and we see that so clearly in the life of the apostles and the early Church. When the apostles met the risen Master, and when they received the Holy Spirit, they could not help but witness to this, to go out and share their experiences and teach about the new life they were filled with. They were in harmony with the culture of God, and when we are in harmony with that, then we allow God to work with us and in us! A wonderful example can be found in the Acts 5:12–16.

Now many signs and wonders were done among the people through the apostles. And they were all together in Solomon's Portico. None of the rest dared to join them, but the people held them in high esteem. Yet more than ever believers were added to the Lord, great numbers of both men and women, so that they even carried out the sick into the streets, and laid them on cots and mats, in order that Peter's shadow might fall on some of them as he came by. A great number of people would also gather from the towns around Jerusalem, bringing the sick and those tormented by unclean spirits, and they were all cured.

Through receiving the Holy Spirit at Pentecost, the disciples were fully in tune with the culture of God, with the mind, the will and heart of the Trinity. The Holy Spirit is, of course, one of the producers of the culture of God. This full harmony manifested itself in their power – even Peter's shadow could now heal people! Even throwing the disciples into prison could not stop them. God acted directly to help them, sending an angel to free them from prison.

> Then the high priest took action; he and all who were with him (that is, the sect of the Sadducees), being filled with jealousy, arrested the apostles and put them in the public prison. But during the night an angel of the Lord opened the prison doors, brought them out, and said, 'Go, stand in the temple and tell the people the whole message about this life.' When they heard this, they entered the temple at daybreak and went on with their teaching.
>
> When the high priest and those with him arrived, they called together the council and the whole body of the elders of Israel, and sent to the prison to have them brought. But when the temple police went there, they did not find them in the prison; so they returned and reported, 'We found the prison securely locked and the guards standing at the doors, but when we opened them, we found no one inside.' Now when the captain of the temple and the chief priests heard these words, they were perplexed about them, wondering what might be going on. Then someone arrived and announced, 'Look, the men whom you put in prison are standing in the temple and teaching the people!' Then the captain went with the temple police and brought them, but without violence, for they were afraid of being stoned by the people. (Acts 5:17–26)

Here, we see that the closer we are to acting according to the will of God, then the more access we have to that power. The culture of God opens the heart of God to those who believe and who want to be in fellowship with this culture.

As the culture of life spread – remember that the angel commanded the disciples to 'tell the people the whole message about this life' – those who heard the disciples' message were liberated from those who tried to control them through their interpretation of the Law. As a result, the temple police began to fear the people because their power was slipping.

> When they had brought them, they had them stand before the council. The high priest questioned them, saying, 'We gave you strict orders not to teach in this name, yet here you have filled Jerusalem with your teaching and you are determined to bring this man's blood on us.' But Peter and the apostles answered, 'We must obey God rather than any human authority. The God of our ancestors raised up Jesus, whom you had killed by hanging him on a tree. God exalted him at his right hand as Leader and Saviour, so that he might give repentance to Israel and forgiveness of sins. And we are witnesses to these things, and so is the Holy Spirit whom God has given to those who obey him.' (Acts 5:27–32)

Here we see that the culture of God is a culture of openness, mercy and forgiveness. God is always open to us, ready to show mercy and to liberate us from any power that takes us away from him. The culture of God is not touched by anger even after Jesus was killed on a tree. The Old Testament often portrays God as showing anger, fury and wrath; the image of a furious God who takes revenge was embedded in the minds of the people at this time. This is what the religious leaders taught, using the anger of God to control the minds and hearts of the people. Here we see a totally different picture of God, free from anger and fury. Even after the horror of the cross, God shows himself through the apostles to be a bringer of reconciliation and forgiveness. God does not hold grudges, fortunately for us all.

The unique experience of Pentecost was shared by Jews and Gentiles alike. But the apostles did not grasp fully what the Holy Spirit was sharing with them. They still thought that they were a movement within Judaism. They were filled with the Holy Spirit and yet they still could not see the truth, blinkered as they were by their own expectations and local culture. So Peter needed another shock.

From birth I was indoctrinated by the state to follow a certain ideology, with a view on who were friends and who were enemies ingrained in my heart. I couldn't see far beyond what had been planted in me. When I went through the Civil War in Lebanon, I was forced to challenge my preconceptions and prejudices, and I was exposed to different ideologies and ways of thinking – but still I resisted. Only when I left the region could I look back and re-evaluate what I had learnt when I was growing up and what I had experienced in the war. I saw the devastating consequences of being indoctrinated as I grew up, and the process of letting go was very painful. My faith and my struggle to understand the culture of God helped me to feel the change in me, and I was no longer afraid to question what I had been taught when I was young. Even blood and tears in the Levant could not enable me to break the barriers that lay within me. It took a fresh life in a new world to melt the barriers like snow inside me under the light of God. Seeking the culture of God helped me to liberate my soul from the bondage of the past and to shake off the chains.

I feel that my experiences resonate strongly with Peter's experience in Joppa. Peter was proud of his upbringing and his religion, and how he practised it, to the extent that he did not hesitate to boast about it even to God.

About noon the next day, as they were on their journey and approaching the city, Peter went up on the roof to pray. He became hungry and wanted something to eat; and while it was being prepared, he fell into a trance. He saw the heaven opened and something like a large sheet coming down, being lowered to the ground by its four corners. In it were all kinds of four-footed creatures and reptiles and birds of the air. Then he heard a voice saying, 'Get up, Peter; kill and eat.' But Peter said, 'By no means, Lord; for I have never eaten anything that is profane or unclean.' The voice said to him again, a second time, 'What God has made clean, you must not call profane.' This happened three times, and the thing was suddenly taken up to heaven. (Acts 10:9–16)

For all of us, we organise our world around ourselves according to what we have been taught, with 'in' and 'out', friends and enemies, right and wrong, values and vices and so on. What a shock when God breaks into our lives and sweeps our ordering of the world aside like a house of cards, and says to us, 'This is not what I want from you.'

When the culture of God reaches us, the inevitable result is that it shakes our world; sometimes it is like a hurricane or an earthquake. We must remember that the disciples had all been raised as Jews, hating the Samaritans and looking down on all 'outsiders', and they found it hard to grasp the consequences of the work of the Spirit when this conflicted with a lifelong obedience to rules of ritual cleanliness.

Despite all his experiences of the universality of the gospel, here is the old Peter, slow to respond to the full implications of Pentecost. In place of the culture of God, he is still proudly stuck in the old Law – dividing the world into those who are 'in' and those who are 'out'. The response of the Lord in the vision reveals the full implications of his culture: 'What God has made clean, you must not call profane.' This encounter is a window into the culture of God, which challenges Peter when he was boasting about his observation of the Law and confronts him with the true nature of the culture of God, which is all-inclusive, celebrating diversity and excluding no one. We know the will of God only through a relationship with him, not through a set of written rules.

diversity

When God reorders our world through our relationship with him, we start to see everything differently. This is what Paul says in his second letter to the Corinthians 5:17: 'So if anyone is in Christ, there is a new creation: everything old has passed away; see, everything has become new!' The culture of God is the new order that we need to adopt. The vision at Joppa equipped Peter for the next shock, although it would still be a mighty shock! When Peter experienced the truly universal nature of God's call to humanity, to be his children, he saw the full and universal implications of his vision at Joppa.

St Luke relates this event with a real sense of urgency and immediacy: 'While Peter was still speaking, the Holy Spirit fell upon all who heard the word. The circumcised believers who had come with Peter were astounded that the gift of the Holy Spirit had been poured out even on the Gentiles, for they heard them speaking in tongues and extolling God' (Acts 10:44–46).

Here is yet another little Pentecost, with all the astonishing signs and impact of the first. St Luke actually says that they 'were astounded that the gift of the Holy Spirit had been poured out even on the Gentiles'. Nothing less than the same signs and symbols as at the first Pentecost would have convinced those who were standing by that the old divisions between Jew and Gentile were abolished and that the gospel was now open to all nations, cultures and languages, reflecting the very culture of God himself.

Peter is like all of us; when we learn the hard way how to adjust to the new order that God brings into our lives, it is not instantaneous. We begin a process of learning, which has its own highs and lows. Meeting the culture of God is a process of transformation throughout our lives, rather than a sudden event. We must remember this with Paul, too. For all his life, from encountering Jesus on the road to Damascus until his beheading in Rome, according to the wide tradition of the Church, Paul continued to grow into the understanding of the culture of God. Along that journey, he would excel and he would also have setbacks. We should always read Paul's writings with a deep consideration of where Paul was on this journey of adaptation at the time he wrote each letter.

The apostles definitely struggled to determine the guidance of the Holy Spirit when it came to thorny issues to do with the Law of Moses and to what extent believers should observe the Law without losing their freedom in Christ. Paul and Peter both worked hard to find the distinction between the culture of God – which was a gift of God to the believers – and the heritage of the apostles, which was the culture of the Law. It was not easy for them to embrace the freedom that the culture of God gave them while simultaneously letting go of the restrictions of the Law, which had played such a huge part in their lives. A lot of Jews who had become Christians were still following the Law of Moses and they believed that you could only become a true Christian if you also kept that Law. They were understandably afraid to abandon what they had grown up with. The culture of God is a whole, and complete, but many have mistakenly tried to add in their own cultures, just as many of the Jewish Christians did.

Today, indigenous Christians in the Levant, who live as a minority, are heavily influenced by the faith and culture of the majority. I remember when I was a child that Christians unconsciously used to treat the Bible like the Muslims treated the Qur'an. For example, they observed the holiness of the Qur'an, which must be treated by Muslims with reverence and cleansing rituals, and they tried to imitate this because, unconsciously, they wanted to show that the Bible was not less than the Qur'an. Many Christians in the Middle East are circumcised because the majority does this. A good number of Christians also speak about reward and punishment after death, where you will be judged according to your works – which is an Islamic belief, not Christian.

It is so difficult to point at these practices and say that they are not Christian – how do you tell someone that they have 'got their faith wrong', possibly for their whole lives?

The dilemma of the early Church is still in the Levant today. In the West, the secular world has also permeated Christian beliefs, especially the Enlightenment and its focus on reason, which pushed Christianity into becoming an intellectual exercise, losing the warmth of the heart. Spirituality is now left to those on the verges of faith.

The apostles had the courage to face these issues, the encroachments of the old ways of the Law, because they relied on the guidance of the Holy Spirit. It is wonderful to read in Acts 15:28 the words of the apostles: 'For it has seemed good to the Holy Spirit and to us to impose on you no further burden than these essentials.' They also relied on their own personal experiences of the Holy Spirit, especially Peter in his observation that the culture of God unconditionally included the Gentiles:

> After there had been much debate, Peter stood up and said to them, 'My brothers, you know that in the early days God made a choice among you, that I should be the one through whom the Gentiles would hear the message of the good news and become believers. And God, who knows the human heart, testified to them by giving them the Holy Spirit, just as he did to us; and in cleansing their hearts by faith he has made no distinction between them and us.' (Acts 15:7–9)

The life of the apostles teaches us much about the nature of the culture of God: that it liberates us from the chains of our earthly cultures and empowers us to discern what is godly in our lives – and what is not. How much do we have the courage to say today that 'It seemed good to the Holy Spirit and to us'? Many Christians still seek refuge in the law to justify themselves or to condemn others – or even to win an argument. Bible verse quoting to intimidate others is not a reflection of the culture of God!

The world of the Levant today, although very different in some ways from the Levant at the time of the apostles, still faces very similar challenges and problems.

Having lived, and grown up, in that very region where Jesus himself lived and grew up, and where Peter and Paul and all the apostles formed their faith and taught it to the world, I have seen that people in that region, more than anywhere else, still fall into the trap of 'If you do not believe like me, then you are condemned by God.' The war in Lebanon, the Arab–Israeli Wars, the long and bloody wars in Iraq and Syria, show us that people are still fragmented; each group believes that they have the only truth and that all others are in the wrong. How have we not learnt to live peacefully together and build our societies, using God's story within that region as a light and a guide? Even when the region was Christian, it was still constantly at war. What God struggled with in the person of Christ in the first century, he is still struggling with today.

So how important is the Holy Spirit to us today? The timeless words of the Metropolitan Ignatius of Lattakia in his address to the Assembly of the World Council of Churches in 1968 puts this challenge most starkly:

Without the Holy Spirit, God is far away
Christ stays in the past,
The Gospel is a dead letter,
The Church is simply an organisation,
Authority is a matter of domination,
Mission is a matter of propaganda,
The liturgy is no more than an evocation,
Christian living a slave morality.

But in the Holy Spirit:
The cosmos is resurrected and groans with the birth
   pangs of the Kingdom,
The risen Christ is here
The Gospel is the power of life,

The Church shows forth the life of the Trinity,
Authority is a liberating service,
Mission is a Pentecost,
The liturgy is both memorial and anticipation,
And human action is deified.

IO

The Culture of God Today: Diversity and Freedom

The letter to the Hebrews (13:8) says that 'Jesus Christ is the same yesterday and today and for ever.' This important statement can also be said about the culture of God, which is the same yesterday, today and forever because it is not limited by the changes of time and space to which we are all subject. But the culture of God is also dynamic, lively and creative, because this culture is the product of the eternal Trinity, which is the Creator and the Sustainer of the whole universe. How can the culture of God be both dynamic and unchangeable? The culture of God is dynamic because there is always interaction between Father, Son and Holy Spirit, which suggests a dynamic dimension. Because we are limited in time and space, we understand change within those limitations. But when we take into account that the dynamic relationship within the Trinity takes place outside the limitations of space and time, then the concept of change takes on a completely different meaning. For example, before the Resurrection, God did not have the man Jesus, but after the Ascension, Jesus the risen man, with his glorified body, was lifted to God; at that point, God changed by receiving the risen Lord. Looking at the culture of God today is extremely exciting because we are seeing the impact of an eternal culture on a constantly changing world.

The world in which we live has gone through radical, enormous changes since the time of Christ. In just the last quarter of a century, our world moved from communicating through landline telephones and a handful of television channels to the crazy, mind-bending revolution of the digital world – which may well be just in its infancy; we have no idea where this revolution will take us. I remember very well when my family got a telephone installed in our home in 1978. The excitement this brought to our lives was immense. In Syria, we first had black-and-white TVs in the 1970s. By the time I was writing my PhD thesis in Germany in the 1990s, I had my first home computer and my first mobile phone. Today, I am the same person, who was once so excited by a basic telephone or a simple black-and-white television, who now takes for granted swiping my finger across a digital screen to send a message instantly around the world, or selecting any of thousands of movies to watch wherever I am. Moving from childhood to adulthood, part of my culture has changed so much that it is unrecognisable. Information which was once the source of incredible power and available only to a few, is now on hand around the clock for everyone. The question now is not what we know, but what to do with the knowledge we have, and how to cope with the changing nature of this knowledge.

Despite all this progress of information and technology, we have more refugees today than at any time since the Second World War, and more tragedies and bloodshed as well. The Levant, especially, the region where God chose to live when he became one of us, has the highest number of refugees and deaths caused by war and violence in the world. We are experiencing the most aggressive wave of religious fanaticism globally today since the Middle Ages. Yet at the beginning of this century – or this millennium – many thought-leaders and even religious leaders believed that the salvation of the world was in the hands of science and scientists. God was losing his throne to reason. We almost declared our brain as our God, which can solve any problem and bring us happiness. In the West, faith was apparently in decline, and secularism, based on atheistic anti-religious principles, was seen to have 'won' the day for humanity; this started to leak into the East and even into the Levant – where people still valued faith most highly in their lives.

We were almost intoxicated with our achievements and we felt that we were unstoppable. Then, on 11 September 2001, the world was changed forever. Not only did the attacks take place on the soil of the United States, but in and around New York, perhaps the ultimate symbol of human material achievement. With its towering skyscrapers, the global financial powerhouse of Wall Street, the massive department stores where anything could be bought, and the glamour of Broadway and Times Square, New York was the dream destination for everybody and it represented a brave new world.

On 9/11, this city would experience acts of violence that changed the world permanently. Thousands of people were killed and many thousands more were injured; the shockwave engulfed the whole planet. I was not shocked or even surprised, though, because I knew that the Levant was boiling with resentment towards the Western world and that Islamic religious fanaticism was growing at a pace we had not seen for many centuries. All this was an ideal pretext for what happened in New York. The fire burning in the Near East sent sparks of sectarianism around the world, starting fresh fires in every country.

The events of 9/11 brought even more bloodshed and violence to the Levant. Just like kicking a fire, the result was an even greater outpouring of sparks. What happened in New York was just one of the sparks, and even today the skies are still thick with the embers of hatred. What we had not learnt was that extreme ideologies cannot be fought with bullets, because such ideologies are based on glorifying dying and killing, promoting a culture of death as offering a shortcut to God's paradise, which the Islamic jihadis see as a place of bodily, physical, and especially sexual pleasure. Sadly, many Islamic religious and political leaders exploited this ideology of death and brainwashed hundreds of thousands of young people, convincing them that the way to paradise, the way to please God, is to destroy the earthly cultures of the infidels (those who do not believe as they do). Their aim is to dominate the world, and bring what they think is the will of God to rule our lives; in this way, they believe that they are making the world live the 'culture of God' on earth. Tragically, those people are blinded to the true will and culture of God. What is happening is that the extremists are being selective in their religion, choosing texts within Islam that could encourage violence against those who could be labelled as 'blasphemers' – *kuffar* in Arabic. This label does not only apply to Christians or Jews or people of any other faiths; it is also applied to other Muslims who do not believe in the same way as the extremists. Not only did the result of this fanaticism devastate non-Muslims in the region and beyond; the hatred and violence has been especially aimed at other Muslims.

We have failed to stop this madness of Islamic fanaticism and sectarianism through war and even through standing together and exposing the sick ideologies, helping young people to see the culture of life that truly is at the heart of every religion or faith. Many Muslims are polarised by the increasing division between the Sunni and Shi'a denominations within Islam, and this is preventing Islam from speaking out against extremism with a common voice. It is not enough to condemn extremism and say that 'This does not represent Islam as a religion.' We all need to stand up and act to bring an alternative religious enlightenment to the lives of young people around the world.

The wars and the bloodshed in the Levant have shattered the trust between the different religious and cultural groups there, profoundly damaging the very fabric of society. The majority Muslims have suffered greatly, and the minorities in the Levant have suffered persecution, displacement and hate crimes. The number of Christians in Syria, Iraq, Lebanon and Palestine has decreased dramatically, as they felt that they were no longer welcome in their homelands, betrayed by their neighbours, and many of them have left for a safer life elsewhere.

The Levant has entered into a long struggle to define where

the Peace of God comes from, and today this struggle continues. In the Lebanese Civil War, the Christian militia understood peace as military victory achieved by death and violence rather than through seeking the peace that is found in the culture of God. Many of them were convinced that their very existence as Christians in Lebanon depended on 'winning the war', although this was based on a total manipulation of religion and faith for political gain. Many sides in the wars in Syria and Iraq, and even in the unsettled political situation in Lebanon, have tried to convince the Christians to support them in the name of 'protection' or 'freedom of religion', but in practice the region has never enjoyed that true freedom of religion, faith and belief, and the Christians never got their peace. In the Levant, Christians have always lost whenever conflict erupts – and the proof is the massive emigration of Christians from the region.

This leads me to look in depth at what Jesus said to his disciples after the Resurrection, when he appeared to them in the upper room. He greeted them with the words, 'Peace I leave with you; my peace I give to you. I do not give to you as the world gives. Do not let your hearts be troubled, and do not let them be afraid' (John 14:27). This magnificent statement is a direct access to the heart of the culture of God, which says absolutely clearly and directly that the culture of God is peace. Then Jesus qualifies that peace, because we often confuse 'peace' with an absence of war. We think we can have either peace or war. But Jesus highlights that what we in the world may understand as 'peace' would not necessarily be how the culture of God would define it. What is the difference? Most of the time, when we talk about peace in the world, we are talking about politics; we speak of negotiating peace, a peace process and peace treaties. But we do not always as a result experience the peace that brings a truly better life. This is the inner peace that we all should possess; peace with creation, with my neighbour and with God.

When Jesus says, 'my peace I give to you', he is referring specifically to the peace that comes to us from following him as our

Lord and Saviour, the perfect example of life and living. The peace that Jesus Christ gives is a life lived in fellowship with the culture of God; it is what St Paul said, 'Let the same mind be in you that was in Christ Jesus' (Philippians 2:5). Enjoying the depth of the peace of Christ means having the mind that was in Jesus. It is the art of following him and 'put[ting] on the Lord Jesus Christ' (Romans 13:14) as Paul says – this is a typical Levantine expression and analogy! Putting on somebody might seem like a strange idea, but it means to have a direct contact with Jesus, wrapping yourself up in him all the time and having the same mind that was in him. This is just like putting on the culture of God, which defines how we think and how we act. Soldiers and police officers put on special clothes that reinforce the qualities needed for those jobs. If you put on fancy dress, you will almost inevitably be affected, directly or subconsciously by it. Clothes change how others see us, but they also change how we see ourselves, and the result is that we are different. Putting on even a cheap plastic crown will give the wearer delusions of nobility and he or she will behave differently – even their posture will change.

The evil of war and violence that we face today is not much different from the situation that Jesus found himself in, as his people were resisting the occupation of a Western power – the Roman Empire. An essential part of the peace in the Roman Empire was a total submission to the will of Caesar, to the extent of worshipping him as a god. In the fourth century, Christianity became the religion of the Roman Empire and that changed the status of Christians; the danger here was that the peace of Christ was treated as part of the Empire's domain rather than a gift from God. This added an imperial Church bureaucracy that became the 'middle men' between the people and God, and they dispensed the peace, rather than recognising that this peace came freely and directly from God and his culture. In the Middle Ages, the Church felt able to go to war in God's name, and peace became a commodity traded by kings and clerics.

For Christians today, the source of peace should not be the lack of war in Europe for seventy years; nor is peace to be found in extreme secularism that erases God and faith completely. More than ever now, in our hugely diverse world, Christians must rediscover where peace comes from, which is the culture of God. The challenges today are different from any we have faced before. One of our greatest challenges is to be agents of peace in a religiously and culturally diverse world, which is contorted by extreme ideologies that actively oppose any difference or diversity. Even the mainstream political parties in any democratic country disrespect and even despise each other. The culture of God is a call to go back to the essence of peace, which comes from the heart of God. What is this peace? It is that we not only accept the other who is different, but that we rejoice at their difference on every level, and we thank God for these differences because God's great desire is diversity. Look at the stars, flowers, even snowflakes and pebbles – everything natural in creation is different.

Paul expresses this very eloquently when he takes the analogy of the body and its members: 'For as in one body we have many members, and not all the members have the same function, so we, who are many, are one body in Christ, and individually we are members one of another' (Romans 12:4–5). I need to highlight that differences are not measures of quality or value, because, in God, differences are all gifts and they are appreciated. In another of his letters, Paul uses the same analogy, explaining this equal value of the members of the body. Although some members of the body may think they are more important, in fact, they are not more important because the body functions as one, and any dysfunction by one member of the body dramatically affects all other members: 'If one member suffers, all suffer together with it; if one member is honoured, all rejoice together with it' (1 Corinthians 12:26).

This kind of diversity, to which Paul is referring, is a diversity that acknowledges the equal value of each member despite the variety of gifts. It also reflects the positive dependency of each member on the others, and the uniqueness of each member is not diminished by its dependence on the others. That takes us directly to the heart of God, which is the reality of the Trinity: each member of the Trinity is unique, but at the same time in unity with the other two members. God could not have asked us to live in uniformity while he is himself in diversity. God being Trinity in this dynamic, productive, positive and fruitful way inspired me to compare the Tower of Babel with the story of Pentecost. The story of the Tower of Babel tried to find an explanation for the diversity of languages which made communication between peoples difficult. In Babel, the diversity of languages is seen as a curse sent upon those who tried, while all speaking a universal language, to build a tower to reach God. Here, diversity is interpreted as God's punishment, a way to prevent people from understanding each other so that they could never challenge God again. The experience of the multiplicity of languages took an opposite direction in the New Testament in the story of Pentecost, when God – through the Holy Spirit – sent us the message that this diversity is a blessing from God. Through this diversity, we can still be one in him, as the disciples were that day when they could speak and be understood in every language: 'Amazed and astonished, they asked, "Are not all these who are speaking Galileans? And how is it that we hear, each of us, in our own native language?"' (Acts 2:7–8).

Today, even two thousand years later, we still discriminate against each other by race, gender, sexuality, culture, religion, status and ability. Diversity is still one of the great challenges that humanity faces. It seems we have not yet learnt the lesson and we still look down on people who are different; we still have not heard the clear words of St Paul: 'There is no longer Jew or Greek, there is no longer slave or free, there is no longer male and female; for all of you are one in Christ Jesus' (Galatians 3:28).

Solving the challenge of diversity could be an enormous step forward for all nations, to build a better and more peaceful world.

It is everyone's responsibility to stand up against the few who try to divide us and abuse the gift of diversity for political and worldly ends.

If we receive peace from God, then we do not allow ourselves to be manipulated for political purposes, and we are focused on the true giver of peace, who is Jesus Christ, whose peace comes directly from the culture of God – which is the culture of peace. Our existence should not come from supporting a political power – it comes from building relationships with everyone based on love and respect and understanding, which are the signs that we are part of the culture of God. This is what it means to live the culture of God in our own local culture. The culture of God is not an abstract concept; it is a spiritual, social, existential relationship with God and others.

If we are to live the culture of God in our own local culture, we need to make it relevant to our daily lives and really accessible to us – and to others. We must first understand what Jesus' teaching meant within his own culture, which I have covered in earlier chapters, and we must then understand the culture of God in terms of our own culture today, reinterpreting the words of Jesus and his disciples according to our own symbols and images.

For example, many people today have never seen a shepherd in their lives. When Jesus said, 'I am the good shepherd', showing that God is a caring God, he would have been inspired by seeing a shepherd working in the distance. What does the shepherd mean for people in a modern city? First, we must understand the shepherd's role and meaning in the original text and then find an analogy that would be meaningful today – such as the bus driver. A good bus driver cares about his passengers and takes them safely from A to B; this could be the modern 'good shepherd'. Not everyone would understand the shepherd, but everyone knows about bus drivers and the difference between a pleasant and a horrible journey to school or work.

Another example of updating the cultural icons could be the vine and the branches becoming the internet and computers/

smartphones. The incredible success stories of global companies like Apple, Amazon or Facebook always start with one or two people in a little office or bedroom; after a journey of struggles and risk, they achieved enormous success. Could this be the modern mustard seed, from which tiny speck a huge tree grows? Taking the Big Bang theory, the whole universe came out of almost nothing. There are many analogies that we can draw today to reinterpret the words of Jesus in our own imagery.

The culture of God enriches and informs our earthly cultures, and it enhances our understanding of our culture and of each other. Just as Jesus was fully immersed in his earthly culture, we must be likewise; he would not have been able to challenge and transform his earthly culture without loving and understanding it, and truly belonging to it. Today, we must do the same – we must understand and love our culture, we must belong to it, and like Jesus we must serve.

The essence of the diversity that we have been considering, the glue that can hold the members of the body together, and the heart that gives the body life to live, is freedom. The culture of God presents to us a quality of God, which is that of the Creator who created humanity in his image. This does not mean that we look like him, but that we have qualities which God also has; the ultimate quality is love.

The first time I went to the United States, while I was living in Beirut, was to attend a youth conference. One of the tasks that was given to me there was to choose a question and put it to as many attendees of the conference as possible. My question was, 'How do you understand freedom?' I vividly remember that the answer of the great majority of people I asked was that freedom means that 'I can do whatever I want to do.' This answer shocked me. I never understood freedom in this way, even though I had lived through war and under dictatorships that existed all across the Levant. Even though I was not at all free to do whatever I wanted in the Levant, I really struggled to accept this answer. I did not have my own clear answer as to what freedom was at that time, but I rejected this 'whatever I want' approach. I could see that the answer was enormously important but, coming from the Levant, I did not know how to even start understanding a concept like freedom. We were not free there even to think about it. I did not want to associate freedom with the political slogans that were everywhere: the greater the dictatorship, the more the trumpeting of 'freedom' to strip the people of their ability to think rationally about it. Totalitarian states use propaganda to anaesthetise their people to their realities, and these states glorify values such as freedom and democracy. East Germany, a totalitarian state, called itself the German Democratic Republic. War and dictatorships reduce people to little more than drones, programmed by their leaders.

Decades afterwards, and after living in many different cultures, I feel that humanity is still challenged by the concept of freedom, and I still cannot accept the definition I heard in the US that freedom means 'to do whatever I want'. I became aware of the limitation of the choices within freedom; however free we are, the choices are limited. The limitations could be personal, cultural, religious, economic, racial and many others. How do I understand that God, in his infinite love, and out of his culture, which is freedom, created us in his own image? The question that jumps into my mind immediately is, 'Does freedom belong to the image of God in us, and if it does, how can we understand it in the limitations that exist in our world?'

At the time of Christ, the Levant was no different. The region was in turmoil politically, with war and dictatorships blighting the land and its people. Jesus also had to deal with dictatorships and violence. How could he speak about 'freedom' in a time of occupation without being wrongly understood as a political freedom fighter who would call for war against the occupier? The Levant in the twenty-first century is a region that still longs for an experience of freedom.

How did Jesus deal with the subject of 'freedom'? I would like to focus on three verses in the Gospel according to St John, which, for me, form three pillars of understanding the culture of God as the culture of freedom.

The first verse is, 'and you will know the truth, and the truth will make you free' (John 8:32). In this bold statement, Jesus makes a vital connection between freedom and truth. Here we have to ask the question that Pilate asked Jesus during his trial: 'What is truth?' (John 18:38). Jesus doesn't leave us without an answer. He makes another amazing statement – the second pillar – which in fact changed my life: 'I am the way, and the truth, and the life' (John 14:6a). God is, simply, the Truth. In him, the source of existence, everything is understood, explained and without doubt. Without God, there is no existence; God is the reason that our lives are real.

In my teens, I was very close to two friends in Lattakia, and we all were in the Boy Scouts. We used to have a lot of discussions, especially philosophical and existential; we were searching for the meaning of 'truth'. I still remember all the wonderful discussions about this. We were so idealistic! On that journey, I read Jesus' breathtaking statement and I thought to myself, 'Either this man was totally crazy, or he knew what he was talking about.' No one else has ever claimed to be, in himself, the truth. He didn't offer to lead people to the truth, or to know the truth, or even to be truthful; he made himself a synonym for the truth itself. Truth and Jesus are interchangeable. This claim changed the course of my life. Today, I still see this statement as a pillar of understanding the concept of freedom. To know the truth, the truth will set us free, means 'to know Jesus Christ, and he will set us free'. This brings us to the third pillar of understanding freedom, which is: 'So if the Son makes you free, you will be free indeed' (John 8:36). In this last statement, Jesus explains that he himself is the way to be free because the freedom he gives us is true freedom.

The meaning we can discern from these pillars is that Jesus is saying that he is the truth, and knowing that the ultimate truth is God, we can see that Jesus is God. Jesus is the one who makes us free, which means that true freedom belongs to the culture of God, because what makes us free is the truth, which is God and Jesus.

Looking at freedom from this perspective means that freedom is not 'to do whatever we want'; the true freedom is actually 'to be', not 'to do' – a relationship with the Son sets us free. So what is freedom? It is the art of living in a relationship with Jesus in the culture of God, living with the awareness that we are living in the culture of God, and that the culture of God is ruling our world – therefore we don't need to worry about our choices because our will and the will of God come very close together. Belonging to the culture of God is not the same as 'being good'; many people with no faith are among the best people in the world.

So what is it about, if not 'being good'? It is about maximising our awareness of our belonging to the culture of God, and then everything else will flow from this. The culture of God is in its essence a relational existence of love. We cannot live our faith alone; I cannot stress this too much. A healthy citizenship in the kingdom of God and the culture of God means living in fellowship with each other, just like the disciples after Jesus had left them physically, 'They devoted themselves to the apostles' teaching and fellowship, to the breaking of bread and the prayers' (Acts 2:42). In the Levant, from the time of Christ up to this moment, fellowship belongs to the very essence of society; because fellowship is so strong there, hospitality and generosity have flourished. I cannot remember a week passing without having guests at home as I grew up.

Part of the culture of God being active in our lives is to challenge our faith institutions, reminding us always to learn from the dark chapters in our history so that we continue to reform ourselves in the light of that culture. The institutions of Christianity have passed through some terrible chapters, and we must be brave enough to face our history and learn not to fall into similar traps. We still fall short as Christians around the world when it comes to standing up against the exploiting of our planet and the destruction of our environment. We also fall short in how we stand up against wars and the arms race; our responsibility is not only to provide some humanitarian help to the victims of warfare, but to go beyond that and take a stand, even if we disturb our political systems. The world is facing one of the worst periods since the Second World War; according to the United Nations, more than sixty million people are refugees or internally displaced (refugees within their own country). The Levant, the region where Jesus lived and taught, is facing the worst humanitarian crisis in the world. In the last five to six years, my country, Syria, has seen almost half of its population of twenty-three million become refugees or 'internally displaced'. If we look at the culture of God, we see how short we have fallen in tackling the most significant issues in our world – such as human trafficking, drug abuse, the sexual exploitation of women, and the abuse of religion for worldly ends. We have a long way to go to give the culture of God the place it deserves in our lives and in our broken world.

The culture of God also guides us in our relationships with other faiths. This culture is not an exclusive club for Christians any more than the Holy Spirit was only reserved for the Jewish community after the Resurrection. As the disciples experienced the work of the Holy Spirit among the Gentiles (the outsiders), we must liberate the culture of God from our limited under-standing and the temptation to decide who is 'in' and who is 'out'. The Cross and the Resurrection of Jesus Christ are a universal invitation to all humanity to know God and his culture. For us as believers in Jesus Christ, the culture of God empowers us to exercise its love, generosity and hospitality in our relation-ships with all other faiths and worldviews. Part of the mystery of God, and of his culture, is that we cannot decide who is included and excluded; we are not meant to judge others! In the Levant today, as it was at the time of Jesus, the manipulation of religion for earthly gain is still rife, and it destroys so many young lives. When I go to the region, which I do often, I still see that we are not even close to learning from the generous, loving and hospitable God who keeps calling us to rejoice and celebrate in our differences. I still experience, every time I visit the Levant, the closed-mindedness of many people from all religions who continue to reject and exclude each other based on religious and sectarian identities – including Christians. Until it is fully adopted, the culture of God will always challenge earthly religious culture, stripping it of its claims to represent God's will faithfully and accurately.

St John picks the strongest and most powerful image of God becoming human when he refers to Jesus Christ as 'the Word'. This teaches us, as does Jesus throughout his life, that the culture of God is a culture of dialogue, and this is what we need to carry out in promoting ways to solve our conflicts in the Levant and around the world. The whole Middle East is still going through shameful bloodbaths, whether in Yemen, Libya, Syria, Iraq, the Holy Land or Egypt. Coming from the Levant, I feel that we all should do much more to challenge our political leaders to adopt more peaceful means – especially dialogue – in stopping this horrible bloodshed.

For us, everything in our lives flows from God's love and from his culture. To be equipped and empowered to make the right choices in life that ultimately lead us to an abundant life, we need to make an essential choice, which is to choose Christ. What does that mean? It means acknowledging that everything in our lives flows from that relationship that we freely decide to have with the risen Jesus Christ, the Son of God. When we have made that decision, this forms the basis and the foundation of our dealing with all other choices and decisions in life. This is the biggest difference between a person who has Christ in their lives and someone who does not. We see the culture of God in the choices that Jesus made in his own life, and the decisions that he took.

We might think that doing whatever we want is the real freedom in our lives: the freedom to do good or bad as we will, the freedom to go on holiday, sleep in, get drunk, watch whatever we choose on TV or the internet, as well as the choices that we value such as freedoms of speech, of religion and of politics. Many of our choices depend on money, but we are free to choose. These choices are necessary in life but what is even more necessary is what makes us choose and what our choices do to us. Being in Christ, and knowing that we belong also to the culture of God, opens up to us a new understanding of how to choose and what to choose. Any excessive practice of any choice will have a negative effect on our lives, even eating and drinking. But the more we choose to get close to Christ, the better our quality of life becomes as our choices are enlightened. The ultimate goal in all of our choices is to be happy in life. But being in Christ is to have this inner joy and peace, which does not come from our worldly choice but which empowers us to choose well. Then, worldly choices lose their grip on us and we are free to live life abundantly. This is the quality that Jesus gives us: that we are no longer attached to the strings of our worldly choices. I do not have to drink alcohol to be happy, I don't have to take drugs to be creative, and I don't have to be a celebrity to be accepted by others. More importantly, I don't have to be rich in order to be happy. Money may bring more comfort in life, but never happiness. Being comfortably off does not make you happy. There are so many examples of very rich people with little or no purpose in life. Do not confuse being comfortable with being happy. Having Christ in our life will not necessarily make us comfortable, but it does bring genuine inner joy and peace.

When Jesus said, 'I came that they may have life, and have it abundantly' (John 10:10), he is talking about our life today in the kingdom of God, which is governed by his culture. Freedom is internal, being eternally free in Christ rather than having unlimited menu options in life today. Our freedom is just the start of our journey of being with Jesus eternally, and this is true freedom.

Paul was in the depths of the darkness of prison when he was so free that he shouted, 'Rejoice in the Lord always; again I will say, Rejoice' (Philippians 4:4). Nobody would have this power if he were not liberated inside. It does not matter what happens in our lives; they can imprison us, torture us or kill us, but they cannot remove the peace and the freedom we have in Christ, which is the culture of God. St Paul gives us a wonderful insight into the contribution that the culture of God makes in our lives, especially when we are in our darkest times, when he says,

> Who will separate us from the love of Christ? Will hardship, or distress, or persecution, or famine, or nakedness, or peril, or sword? As it is written, 'For your sake we are being killed all day long; we are accounted as sheep to be slaughtered.' No, in all these things we are more than conquerors through him who loved us. For I am convinced that neither death, nor life, nor angels, nor rulers, nor things present, nor things to come, nor powers, nor height, nor depth, nor anything else in all creation, will be able to separate us from the love of God in Christ Jesus our Lord. (Romans 8:35–39)

Jesus himself lived those dark hours, especially during his trial and crucifixion. God is with us in our darkest hours even if it feels that we are abandoned. The Christians in the Levant today are going through one of the darkest times in their history, and we must remind ourselves that, through this persecution and pain, nothing can separate us from the love of God. We live in his kingdom and his culture. Remember that the kingdom of God (and this could be another book in its own right) is with us here and now in our hearts; it is not a reward for the 'good' in the afterlife. From the second that you believe in Christ, you are in the kingdom of God. We evangelise not to 'save people from hell' but to enable them to taste the kingdom today in their lives. I have seen the work of the culture of God in the lives of young Syrian and Iraqi men and women in the Awareness

Foundation's Ambassadors for Peace programme, when they turned in just a few days from feeling abandoned, devastated and furious with both the world and God, to embracing the power of his culture and, through this power, became a transformative force in their shattered world; they truly are the light in that darkness that surrounds them.

Those young people, as I stood before them, training them to be Ambassadors for Peace, inspired me. I was deeply touched by them because, in their vulnerability, I found hope and a glimpse of how the culture of God is a light in the darkness, a force for change, and a whole world of love to be explored. The young men and women helped me to break my barriers as I was helping them to break theirs. I experienced that, once the culture of God is active in our lives, surprising and unexpected sparks and results and fruits happen. This affirmed that every life can be enlightened and excited, challenged by this culture, the culture of eternal love that gushes from within the heart of the Trinity to drive us forward in our journey of building a world of many cultures ruled by the one culture, which is the culture of the most loving and gracious God.

AFTERWORD:

The Culture of God and Dialogue

War and violence pose the most serious challenge to humanity: how to solve our problems and conflicts without having to annihilate each other.

Violence in the twentieth century manifested itself in the most vicious way in the two world wars, the Korean War, the Spanish Civil War, the Vietnam War, the Israeli–Arab Wars, the extended Lebanese Civil War, the Iran–Iraq War, and then the wars against Iraq, plus many other shameful conflicts around the world, such as the war in Sudan which divided the country into two, the massacres in Rwanda, Nigeria, Myanmar, Cambodia and so many more. It is hard to list all the armed conflicts that stormed across the globe during one single century. The twentieth century, considered to be the beginning of the modern era of technology and science, also marked the serious decline of religion in the West. In this maelstrom of violence, we witnessed – especially in the Levant – the rise of Islamic fanaticism, which grew rapidly and shot its sparks beyond the Levant to reach every country on earth.

One question that we must face is, 'Why are we failing, over and over again, to solve our problems and differences without resorting to violence?' An unavoidable follow-up question is, 'Where is the culture of God in a world that seems bent on self-destruction?' This second question becomes even more critical when we see that we are reckless enough to ignore the fact that we are destroying our planet. Our hostility and short-sightedness seem to reach to everything.

Where is the culture of God? Of course, against this dark and pessimistic view of the world, there have been numerous moments when human beings have reflected the image of God in a glorious form, and there are some who show, or have shown, us that the divine culture is still blooming in the hearts of people. We celebrate the life and service of people like Martin Luther King, Nelson Mandela, Mother Teresa, Dietrich Bonhoeffer, and scientists like Albert Einstein, Stephen Hawking and Georges Lemaître, as well as those who explored the vastness of creation, whether on land, sea, air or in space, or who have brought light and hope to the world through their art, whether in music, painting, sculpture or the written word. These people, and many others, have shone like a beacon in the apparent darkness of our world.

St John opens his narrative of the Gospel by saying that, 'In the beginning was the Word, and the Word was with God, and the Word was God' (John 1:1). The 'Word', which is *logos* in Greek, has a vast series of theological interpretations; many books have been written about the philosophy and theology of 'logos'. What matters to me is that John identified Jesus with the Word, and he went even further to identify God with the Word; this means that when God wanted to send his final message to humanity, his message was nothing less than himself. He was the messenger and the message, the way and the destination, the sea and the harbour. God engaged with humanity absolutely directly – so directly that he became one with humanity in Christ. In him, dialogue took the ultimate and the deepest form, to the extent that, in this dialogue, the two cultures, the culture of God and the earthly culture of Jesus in the Levant, merged in a unity that has had an impact on every human culture ever since.

If God, in his infinite wisdom, chose to highlight so powerfully the role of dialogue, a role that he lived and practised with humanity, isn't it good enough for us to learn how to respect and rejoice in every single life on earth? Isn't it time to find ways to avoid the destruction of life, bringing a final end to wars that consume not only endless innocent lives but also the dignity of our humanity? Looking at the culture of God and how Jesus Christ revealed it in his own time, we see that the heart of his personality, his life and teachings lay in the use of words against hostility, violence and corruption. He even told us to pray for those who persecute us, using words rather than violence as the only way to face evil. Jesus entered into dialogues and debates, he taught in parables and he taught directly; he was always in action, using words. What is so remarkable is that even when Jesus did not speak, when he abstained from words, then his silence was a powerful as his teaching. We see that very clearly in his trial or before he made major decisions. An important role of his silence was to allow others to speak, and to listen to what they had to say; in this way, Jesus could form a proper response that revealed something of the culture of God. We have seen this when he was presented with the woman who was caught in adultery, when he met the Syro-Phoenician woman, and when he took time to pray.

Human differences need exploration, respect, listening and understanding. This is how we come to a better ground for dialogue. I learnt that, when I listen before I speak, and the other person does the same, then we both are able to move to a new area of communication where new opportunities for reconciliation and resolving our differences open up. I know that this works. I have used words alone to persuade armed streetfighters in Beirut to put down their weapons so that they could come and join in our debates; I have persuaded fighters to leave our theology school to protect the lives of those studying within. In my life in the Levant, after having lived through violent regional conflicts that involved many international powers, I could see, looking at this through the lenses of the culture of God that Christ showed us, that what was always lacking was proper, respectful and open dialogue. Even in the peace conferences that I have witnessed over the last thirty years, the vast majority have been based on fighting over selfish interests rather than genuinely seeking a solution that serves the people of the region; this goes against the heart of the culture of God. The people of the Levant have suffered for centuries under military dictators, foreign oppressors, armies of occupation, persecution and even attempts to eliminate our cultures and language. The result of a total lack of political, economic and religious freedom is that the people of the Levant lack the skills of leadership and dialogue that they desperately need today.

Although Jesus was the messenger and the message, we need to understand that the divine dialogue with humanity in Christ existed in both words and in actions. The words and the actions were always hand in hand. Jesus was the Word, but the Word became flesh. Jesus said, 'Pray for those who persecute you' and on the Cross he prayed to his Father to forgive those who were crucifying him, 'for they do not know what they are doing'. The culture of God tells us that the heart and the passion of God is a dynamic and active love that is expressed eternally and continuously in the service of humanity; God is always serving us. If we take this approach, the approach of the Trinity, and we apply it in any region around the world, to seek a dialogue that has love for humanity in its very essence, and the aim of which is to serve humanity, then we would never fail to solve our conflicts through entirely peaceful means. The culture of God is not a theoretical, philosophical, intellectual concept. It is a challenging, transformative and life-changing power that opens up the world to what Jesus called 'abundant life'. Living abundantly is living the life of service that flows from love and respect of humanity. The culture of God teaches us to protect the sanctity of life, which is defiled by war.

Finally, the culture of God is always and everywhere in harmony with our earthly cultures, and this harmony includes affirmation, challenge and an unending invitation to meet in the heart of God, whatever our race, our culture and our religion may be, because the culture of God, the heart of God, is the ultimate space for humanity to fulfil its potential and the purpose of its creation.

Acknowledgements

Living for so many years away from home, Syria, has given me the opportunity to study my original Near Eastern culture closely and understand it more deeply.

I would not have been able to write this book without the support and encouragement of my friend and teacher, the Revd Dr Habib Badr, whose wisdom, love and care inspired me to keep exploring the concept of the culture of God. My special thanks go to Dr George Sabra, the President of the Near East School of Theology, for his incredible dedication to teaching me theology and equipping me to write it too, even when I was a youth leader in Beirut during the Lebanese Civil War. I am indebted to all my teachers and friends along the journey that led me to explore this amazing concept which has enriched and challenged my whole life.

I should like to express my gratitude to the people at two churches for their incredible support and their generous hearts: Holy Trinity Sloane Street, especially the Founding Chair of the Awareness Foundation, Charles Longbottom MBE, the charity's Founding President, the Rt Revd Michael Marshall, Christopher Bunting and Mme Barbara Meynert; and St Nicholas Deptford.

The writing of this book was made possible through the enormous help I received from my friend and colleague at the Awareness Foundation, St.John Wright, who was my first reader and springboard. I am also grateful to all my colleagues at the

Awareness Foundation for their patience during the process of writing.

Finally, my ultimate gratitude goes to the Lord, Jesus Christ, who has blessed me with a wonderful family who have filled my life with joy and love.

I hope that you have enjoyed reading *The Culture of God*, my very first book. There is so much more to say about this fascinating subject. Would you like to receive exclusive content from me? To receive blogs, videos and other exclusive materials, go to www.awareness-foundation.com/nadim-nassar and sign up!

awareness
FOUNDATION

The Revd Nadim Nassar is the Founder and Executive Director of the Awareness Foundation, an ecumenical, educational charity founded in 2003 to empower people of faith to embrace diversity and build peaceful and harmonious communities. We are active in the UK[i], USA[ii], Canada, the Middle East (Syria, Iraq, Jordan, Lebanon and Palestine), and in Hong Kong. **Our Royal Patron is HRH The Countess of Wessex GCVO.**

Through our Little Heroes programme, we have already helped more than 2,000 children in Syria to smile again, to believe in themselves and begin to overcome the great troubles they have faced. We do this through a combination of counselling, play and Bible study. Through becoming Little Heroes, the children can build new bridges of respect and understanding with children of other faiths whom they meet in their new homes and schools.

We have taught over 700 young people to be Ambassadors for Peace in Syria and Iraq, showing them how to handle conflict, how to transform and empower their communities and how to build bridges with other faiths to promote peace and under-standing. The Awareness Foundation is widely recognised for its uniqueness in offering these services, peace-making in the Middle East and strengthening community bonds in the West.

Outside the Middle East, the Foundation helps Christians live their faiths fully and faithfully in this diverse, globalised world through our media programme, PAX. Often featuring Nadim's teaching. PAX encourages Christians to live a confident faith. We also work with other religions to emphasise that an enlight-ened, thoughtful faith that preaches hospitality and generosity is a wellspring of community harmony rather than division.

i Registered Charity in England & Wales, No. 1099873
ii 501©3 non-profit organization, EIN 94-3305814